The

International

Student's Guide

to

Studying in the United States

Holly R. Patrick

WAYZGOOSE PRESS

*The International Student's Guide to Studying
in the United States*
© 2016 Holly R. Patrick

Published in the United States by Wayzgoose Press.
Edited by Dorothy E. Zemach.
Book design by DJ Rogers.

ISBN-10: 1-938757-22-X
ISBN-13: 978-1-938757-22-8

Welcome

Congratulations on being accepted to an institute of higher learning in the United States! As an international student, you join hundreds of thousands of individuals who travel from every corner of the globe each year – from Asia, the Middle East, the Americas, Africa and Europe – to study in the U.S.

Some of you recently graduated from high school and are ready to enter the world of higher education, while others have finished college and are ready to continue studying at the graduate level. Still others are mid-career professionals seeking to build on years of experience in your field through further academic training. Representing a broad range of backgrounds and cultures, you bring insight and experience that contribute to the diversity and richness of academic life in America, both inside and outside the classroom. We are glad you have chosen to study in the U.S., home of some of the best colleges and universities in the world!

As you begin this journey, you are probably full of energy and excitement. Studying in the U.S. is a wonderful opportunity that you have worked long and hard to attain, and the time has finally arrived. At the same time, you may feel somewhat anxious, as this is a completely new experience and you are not sure what to expect. It can be a stressful time; there are many things to do in preparation for the trip, and even more to do after you arrive. There are many unknowns, and lots of questions to be answered.

This guide was created for you, the international student, to answer your questions about all aspects of this great adventure – from preparing for the trip and adapting to the new culture, to succeeding in school and embarking on the next steps in your career. Ultimately, the aim of this book is to provide you with insider information and tips that will facilitate your transition to life as a student in the U.S. and help you successfully reach your personal, academic, and career goals. Welcome!

Table of Contents

UNIT 3 BEING A SUCCESSFUL STUDENT

UNIT 4 Developing Your Career

Part 1 Getting Started 128

Part 2 Selling Yourself 137

UNIT 5 Furthering Your Education

UNIT 1

Getting Ready to Go

Part 1: Getting Started

As you begin making plans for your move to the U.S., you want to make sure the transition goes smoothly. Get started early and take advantage of the time before you leave. This section will let you know what to do before you leave to get off to a good start in your new home.

Here you will find information and tips on:

- Learning about Your School
- Financing Your Education
- Obtaining Your Immigration Documents
- Making Living Arrangements
- Creating a Budget
- Improving Your English
- Packing Your Bags

Learning about Your School

The more you know about your school before you arrive, the more comfortable you will be during your first days on campus. Fortunately, practically all information about a school, its programs, and its faculty is available on a school's website. Schools are experienced at anticipating students' questions, so they put information in one, easily accessible place. You will be expected to look at your school's website regularly to find information you need, so start making that a habit right away.

One of the most important web pages to look at carefully is the school's *Office of Student and Scholar Services*. This site has critical information specifically for international students on a number of topics, including maintaining your immigration status while in the U.S. You should also be aware of key dates on the academic calendar, including:

- New student and/or international student orientation
- Deadline for registering for classes
- Start of classes
- Deadline for withdrawing from/adding classes
- Last day of classes
- Final exam schedule

Campus Resources

All schools in the U.S want students to succeed, so they provide resources to help support students academically, emotionally, socially, and professionally. Students usually do not have to pay extra for these services, as the cost is included in the tuition. On the school's website, you can find information about resources such as:

Tutoring Services

Tutors provide students with one-on-one instruction in a variety of academic subjects.

Writing Center

Writing centers offer one-on-one tutoring services as well as workshops on academic writing skills.

 tip You will spend a lot of time typing papers in school, so make sure your typing skills are in good shape!

International Programs Office

Many schools have offices that provide programs and services especially for international students.

Career Center

The career center can be one of the most important resources on campus. This office offers information and guidance on pursuing employment opportunities, such as: resume and cover letter writing instruction, career counseling, job fairs, mock (practice) job interviews, job listings, and networking events.

IT Support

The office of information technology supports the students' computing resources, including computer labs and email services.

Counseling Center

These offices offer one-on-one and/or group counseling for students who would like help managing feelings of homesickness, anxiety, depression, and stress.

Office of Religious Life

This office provides programs and services for students of many faiths who wish to be engaged in spiritual life while in the U.S.

Women's Center

Many schools have a center offering programs that support women on campus, including developing leadership skills and working for gender justice.

LGBT Resource Office

An LGBT (Lesbian, Gay, Bisexual, and Transgender) resource office provides programs and services that support students of all sexual orientations, gender identities, and gender expressions.

Office of Disability Services

This office provides services such as test accommodations and note-taking services to students with disabilities.

Student Organizations

One of the advantages of being a student in the U.S. is the opportunity to participate in student organizations on campus. An enormous variety of clubs exists in colleges and universities around the country, including academic and honor societies, cultural and political groups, media and arts clubs, religious groups, and social service organizations. Many international students also participate in student government, which comprises students elected to represent the interests of the entire student body.

Greek Life

Fraternities and sororities are organizations of mostly undergraduate students (men and women, respectively). Typically, the names of these groups are made up of Greek letters, such as ΣΝ (Sigma Nu) and ΔΣΘ (Delta Sigma Theta).Each society has its own symbols and traditions. Members participate in social activities and community service, and most groups have a local chapter house on campus that provides residential and dining facilities for members. Chapters of the same fraternities and sororities exist on college campuses throughout the US, and thus provide members with access to a broad community. International students are welcome to join.

Sports and Recreation Facilities

Most U.S. schools have sports and recreation facilities where students can exercise and have fun. Often there is an extra fee associated with use of the gym, although sometimes this is folded into the general tuition charge. Schools also support club and team sports such as football, basketball, baseball, soccer, and table tennis.

Financing Your Education

Upon being accepted to a school in the U.S., international students must submit evidence of financial resources equal to or exceeding the costs of the first year of studies. Because the cost of tuition, books and living expenses can be steep, careful financial planning is needed to ensure that you will have the funds to complete your program of study.

While international students are not eligible for U.S. federal aid, there are others sources of funding. However, finding funding resources requires a great deal of time, effort, and organization. If you are looking for loans, grants, or scholarships, allow plenty of time for searching, applying, and receiving the funds, and keep records of all your applications. It is a good idea to apply to as many as scholarships as possible and be determined. Here are some places to look:

Online Scholarship Databases

There are a number of sites on line where you can find information on scholarships available to international students. Search for "scholarships for international students."

Your Government

The government in your home country may be a source of funding. Be aware, however, that there may be stipulations involved in the offer of grants or loans; for example, you may be required to return home to your country to work in a particular field or agency after earning your degree.

Your Employer

Some companies offer benefits that include covering all or part of the costs of earning an advanced degree. If you are currently working, it is worth finding out if this type of program exists at your company.

Sponsoring Organizations

There are several international organizations that grant scholarships to students all over the world; information can be found online. Some organizations sponsor students from particular parts of the world, while others focus on specific populations of students – such as women or citizens of developing countries – so it is worth researching programs for which you may qualify. Check the website of the U.S. embassy in your country to see what scholarships are currently available for international students.

Your School

Many U.S. colleges and universities offer a limited number of merit-based scholarships. The deadlines for these scholarships are often early in the admissions process, so it is a good idea to check the dates online. Also, while public schools (state universities) rarely offer a tuition discount, private schools sometimes have this option for students in particular need.

International Student Loans

International students are eligible for private international student loans to study in the United States. However, to be approved for a loan, you must attend a participating school and have a U.S. citizen or permanent resident with good credit who has lived in the U.S. for the past two years co-sign the loan for you. A co-signer is legally obligated to repay the loan if the borrower fails to pay.

If you take out loans to pay for school, you will have to pay the money back plus interest. The interest rate is based on your co-signer's creditworthiness. If your loan application is approved, you will be informed of the interest rate to be charged, at which point you can accept or refuse the loan. The most important factors to consider when considering taking out loans are: the total amount of the loan with interest, how much the monthly payments will be, and when re-payments will begin.

The decision to take out large loans requires serious consideration; be careful about taking on too much debt. If you do borrow money for school, it is a good idea to borrow only what you need to cover your costs.

Employment

Many students want to work while in school. However, immigration regulations are very strict regarding working on a student visa. The most common status for full-time international students, F-1 status, allows for part time, on-campus employment (fewer than 20 hours per week). Students on a J-1 visa face similar restrictions and must receive permission to work from the program sponsor. While working on-campus can help with expenses, these jobs typically do not pay very much; you can expect to earn around $5,000 per academic year with an on-campus job. In addition, you should consider the effect that working part-time could have on your ability to study and complete assignments.

Obtaining Your Immigration Documents

To enter the U.S, you will need a student visa. The student visa processing times can from a few weeks to a few months, so don't wait to submit your application.

The two most common types of student visas are the F-1 and the J-1.

- An F-1 visa permits international students to pursue education (academic studies and/or language training programs) in the United States
- A J-1 visa permits visitors participating in programs that promote cultural exchange to obtain training in the U.S. J-1 students must be sponsored either by a private or government program.

To get a visa, you must obtain a *certificate of eligibility for non-immigrant student status* from the school to which you have been accepted – this will be either Form I-20 or Form DS-2019. The I-20 or DS-2019 you receive will include your Student and Exchange Visitor Information System (SEVIS) student tracking number. With this number, you must go online to:

1) Pay the SEVIS fee

2) Fill out the visa application forms

3) Schedule your visa interview

When you go to the U.S. embassy or consulate for the visa interview, make sure to take your I-20 orDS-2019 form and SEVIS receipt.

In the visa interview, be prepared to:

- provide information about yourself, including your academic background and the school/program to which you have been admitted
  demonstrate your English language skills
- provide proof of your ability to support yourself financially while living in the U.S.

The interviewer may ask questions about your school and why you chose that particular institution. Be prepared to show that you did your research to find the best school based on your goals and financial resources.

> **tip** There is no reason to pay an agency to help you get a student visa; avoid any agency that claims to provide this service.

Making Living Arrangements

One of the most important tasks you need to accomplish before your trip is finding a place to live. Because this process can take time, you should begin as soon as possible. You can either live on or off campus, depending on your preference and the rules and options of your particular school. In any case, you want to know that you have a place where you feel safe and comfortable.

Dormitories

U.S. colleges and universities generally provide undergraduate students with housing on campus in buildings called *dormitories (dorms)*. In fact, some schools require at least first-year undergraduate students to live in dorms. If you are going to live on campus, the school will work with you to make those arrangements and match you with one or more roommates. The size, appearance, and amenities of dorms vary widely among campuses, but living in a dorm offers a unique opportunity to make friends and engage in campus life.

Off-campus Housing

While some schools offer housing for graduate students, others do not, so many graduate students and some undergraduates live off campus – usually in apartments, but sometimes in shared rental houses. Like dorms, the size, appearance and amenities of off-campus housing vary widely. However, living off-campus offers students a bit more freedom and more opportunities to experience life outside of school. Living off-campus opens up a range of options, so it is a good idea to think about what your priorities are.

Some things to consider are:

- Do you need to pay a deposit?
- How much is the rent?
- Does the rent include any utilities?

- What day of the month is the rent due?
- What happens if you are late paying the rent?

> **tip**
>
> Don't rent an apartment you can't afford. Rent will be your largest monthly expense, so it's important to rent an apartment in your budget. That may mean living in a place without all the amenities – e.g., swimming pool, gym, 12-foot ceilings. Aim for the most affordable place that meets your needs for comfort and safety.

- **Furnishings:** Is the apartment furnished or unfurnished? If it is furnished, what are the furnishings?

- **Laundry Facilities:** Is there a washer and a dryer in the apartment? If not, is there a laundry room in the apartment complex/building, or a Laundromat nearby?

- **Security Deposit:** Is a security deposit required to move in? If so, how much is it, and how do you get it back?

> **tip**
>
> Most apartments ask for a security deposit when you sign the lease equal to one or two months' rent. If you keep your apartment clean and undamaged, you should get that money back when you move out. Make sure to point out to the landlord anything that is damaged or broken when you move in, so you will not be responsible for the damage when you leave.

- **Lease:** How long is the lease (rental contract)? Six months? One year? What happens if you want to move out before the lease ends?

- **Utilities** (e.g., water, electricity, gas, Internet): Is the cost of utilities included in the rent? If not, how much are they each month typically? How do you get the services connected?

- **Cable TV:** Is cable service included in the rent? If included, what company is used? How much is the monthly fee?

- **Proximity/Transportation to Campus:** Is the apartment close to campus? How do students usually get to campus? Is parking available? If so, is there a fee for parking?

- **Security:** What kind of security measures are there to keep residents safe?

Another key question is: "When can I move in?" If you arrive in the U.S. before the move-in date, you will have to find a temporary place to stay, such as a hotel, which can be expensive and inconvenient.

> **tip**
>
> Many students choose to live with one or more roommates and share expenses; schools often provide assistance finding roommates. Other resources include social media sites of international student groups and the websites of the apartment complexes.

Creating a Budget

Being a student usually means living on a limited budget. In the U.S., this is true for domestic and international students alike. As part of your preparations, therefore, create a budget that lists your monthly income and expenses, including rent, utilities, food, and entertainment. The process of making a budget will help you think about what you *want* versus what you *need*. Because you don't know exactly what your expenses will be at first, it's a good idea to overestimate them; you can always adjust downward later. The most important thing is to be realistic.

In making a budget, it's important to have a system for tracking and organizing your financial information. There are mobile apps and Internet sites for this if you don't want to use paper.

Make sure to track your spending routinely; as you do, you'll have a good idea of where your money is going. Tracking everything you make and spend may sound like a lot of work, but it is important to know you exactly what you're spending on; you may realize that you're spending more than you thought.

You should also prepare for the unexpected by building an emergency fund. You can do this by including savings as a recurring expense item in your monthly budget. Saving some money each month will help you cover unusual expenses and plan for changes that may happen while you're in school, such as moving from a dorm to an apartment or buying new clothes for an internship.

Because living on a tight budget is tough, here are some tips:

- **Set limits.** Give yourself a set amount of cash for entertainment or groceries each week to keep yourself on track.
- **Keep credit card purchases to a minimum**. Credit cards make it easy to spend a lot on things you don't need, so avoid using them too often. Also, to avoid paying interest and creating debt, never charge more on a card than you can afford to pay each month.
- **Use your student discount**. Nowadays, in addition to discounts at movie theaters, museums and restaurants, many retail stores offer student discounts on everything from clothes to computers.
- **Buy used items.** Practically everything people have used is on sale again either by the individual, online, or in a store – everything from clothes to furniture to textbooks. Some students even rent textbooks from used textbook websites.

Be aware that, in most states in the U.S., a state sales tax will be added to the price of all goods and services you purchase. Rates vary by state, and in addition to state tax, counties and cities may add their own tax as well.

Improving Your English

For students whose first language is not English, the opportunity to improve your English language skills is one of the advantages of studying in the U.S. Through daily interaction with native English speakers and ongoing exposure to the language, your English proficiency will certainly increase. However, the better your ability to communicate in English is when you arrive in the U.S., the easier it will be to make the adjustment and feel comfortable in your new surroundings. Two of the most important things you can do to enhance your English skills are: read materials and watch videos in English.

Reading Materials in English

Reading is one of the best ways to expand your vocabulary. It is especially important to read English language materials other than textbooks, so that you are exposed to authentic, formal, and informal language. Reading magazines, websites, and newspapers also provides the opportunity to learn about current events and issues of interest in the U.S. In addition, if you pay attention to grammar, word choice, and other aspects of the language while you read, you can use those materials as models for your own writing. Many ebook retail sites such as Amazon and iBook's offer hundreds of novels for free. These can be read on a computer, a tablet, or a smartphone.

Watching Videos in English

Watching TV series, movies, or online videos in English goes a long way to help you understand everyday spoken English. Americans' speech is often full of slang (very informal speech) and varies greatly in terms of accent, speed, and clarity. International students with experience listening to a variety of native English speakers generally have an easier time understanding Americans when they arrive in the U.S. In addition, just like reading magazines and newspapers, watching the news, TV series, or other programs online will help you become more familiar and comfortable with American culture.

Intensive English Programs (IEPs)

Hundreds of U.S. educational institutions offer intensive English programs (IEP). Courses may be taken to prepare for U.S. college or university admission, and some IEPs offer "bridge programs" that help students gain sufficient English proficiency to transfer into an academic program. IEPs usually offer a number of levels of English as a Second Language (ESL) classes, from beginning to advanced, and require 20-30 hours per week of intensive language study.

If the school to which you are admitted has an IEP program, the staff there may assess your English skills and, if necessary, require you to take language courses before the enrolling in an academic degree program. If your school does not have an IEP, and you are interested in studying English in the U.S. before enrolling in a full-time degree program, research your options to find a program that best fits your needs. The Institute of International Education publishes an annual directory of Intensive English Language Programs in the United States, which can be found online. Select a program that is accredited by the Accrediting Council for Continuing Education and Training (ACCET) or the Commission on English Language Program Accreditation (CEA).

Pronunciation

Accurate pronunciation helps you be understood when you interact with others in the U.S. However, for most international students, native-like pronunciation in English can be difficult to achieve for a couple of reasons. First, accurate pronunciation not only involves individual sounds, but also sentence stress, intonation, word linking, rhythm, and word stress. Second, after many years of speaking a second language, a person's pronunciation becomes a fairly well-established habit. This is known as fossilization, and it takes quite a bit of work to change, especially for adult learners. Likewise, many language learners cannot hear the distinct sounds in the second language and, therefore, are unsure how to make them. Given the challenges, to be easily understood, rather than to achieve native-like pronunciation, is often a more realistic goal. To do this, spend as much time as possible interacting with native speakers, making a point to listen to and imitate their pronunciation.

Packing Your Bags

Because your stay in the U.S. is long term, you won't be packing light. The good news is that whatever you cannot manage to fit in your luggage, you can probably purchase when you arrive. The most common items to pack are computers and other electronic devices, health and hygiene products, photos, and of course, clothes. Different events and environments call for different types of dress, so either bring or plan to buy both formal and informal clothing. Here are some examples of style of clothing you will need:

- **Casual:** Typically jeans or shorts in the summer. Unless your school indicates otherwise, casual attire is usually acceptable for going to class.

- **Business Casual:** Dressed-up versions of casual clothes. For men, it means pants (not jeans) and a collared shirt with or without a jacket. For women, it means a nice blouse with a skirt or dressy pants. At school, you may be asked to wear business casual attire for something like a class presentation.

- **Business/Professional:** Suits and ties for men; and suits, conservative dresses, or conservative skirts and blouses for women. This style is appropriate for a career fair or job interview.

Because the U.S. is such a large country, it is home to a number of different climates; the weather where your school is will determine what kind of clothing you will need. In general, areas of the U.S. have these climates:

- **Midwest:** The Midwest region is moderately dry with four distinct seasons, ranging from mild summer months to very cold winter months.

- **Northeast:** Summers in the Northeast are usually pleasant, sunny, and warm, but in the winter, the region often experiences heavy snow and freezing rain.

- **Northwest:** The Northwest is the wettest part of the country. Temperatures remain mild throughout the year, and fog and light drizzle are common.

- **Southeast:** The Southeast region is mostly hot and humid during the summer, and while it can get cold, this region has milder temperatures in the winter than other parts of the country.

- **Southwest and California:** The hottest region of the United States, the Southwest, has a desert climate. California has a milder, Mediterranean-like climate, with wet winters and dry summers.

> Because of high air conditioning, places like classrooms, restaurants, and movie theaters can be quite cold in the U.S.in the summer, so it is a good idea to wear layers of clothing.

In the U.S., temperature is measured in degrees Fahrenheit. Generally speaking, the temperature in Fahrenheit can be thought of like this:

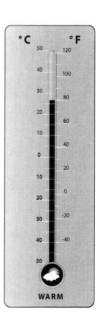
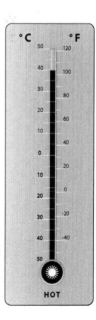

Pack at least a couple of months of any medications you are taking, and if you have children who will be enrolled in school, bring their immunization records (translated into English if necessary). Also, make copies of important documents and leave them with friends or family at home in case the originals are lost.

> Find out what your options are for getting from the airport to your school or apartment (e.g., taxi, shuttle, subway) or arrange for a pick-up before you leave. Some schools offer airport pick-up for international students.

It's a good idea to pack items you need for the first couple of days in your carry-on bag, in case your checked baggage doesn't arrive when you do!

If possible, exchange some of your local currency for U.S. dollars before you leave, so you will have cash with you when you arrive. You might need cash to pay for taxis, meals, and other expenses during your first few days. Depending on your bank, you might not be able to withdraw cash from an ATM (automatic teller machine). You might also need some cash to set up a new bank account in the U.S.

tip

Familiarize yourself with U.S. currency before you arrive. Bills come in denominations of: $1, $5, $10, $20, $50, $100 and up. Here are the most common coins:

| Quarter | Dime | Nickel | Penny |

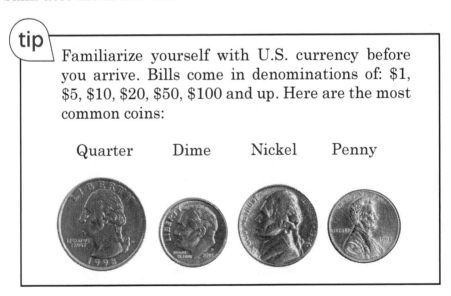

Part 2: Settling In

Upon arriving in the U.S., there are a few things you will need to do to get settled in, such as getting the electricity turned on, finding transportation, and buying groceries. Knowing what you need to do in advance will help you get off to a good start. This section will let you know what to do when you first arrive to make yourself at home. Here you will find information and tips on:

- Setting Up Services
- Arranging for Transportation
- Furnishing Your Home
- Living with Roommates

Setting Up Services

Cell Phone

You will want your cell (mobile) phone service activated as soon as possible, so you can give a local phone number to school staff and students, as well as your bank, landlord, and others with whom you do business. There are a number of companies to choose from, depending on where you are in the U.S., and their plans for calling and text message services vary. Major U.S. cell phone companies include: AT&T, Sprint, Verizon, and T-Mobile. If possible, go to the store in person to talk with a representative about your particular service needs. It's also helpful to ask other students which provider they use. Because you will not have a social security number, you might have to pay on a month-to-month basis or pay a deposit up front.

> **tip**
>
> Americans will expect to be able to leave a message on your phone if you do not answer, so set up your voicemail system as soon as your phone is activated.

Internet

Like cell phone service, there are a number of Internet companies to choose from, depending on where live, and their plans vary; so again, you'll need to talk with a company representative about your particular needs, and ask residents in your area which provider they use.

Utilities, Internet, and Cable TV

If you are living off campus, you will need to set up utilities, such as water and electricity. The individual or company that manages the property can tell you which services you need to set up and which company provides each service. In some apartments or shared homes, the cost of utilities and other services is included in the rent; but in others, payments for these services are made directly to the service provider.

Enrolling Children in School or Daycare

Many international students bring their spouses and children to the U.S. Parents can take care of infants and toddlers at home, or pay for daycare at a center or private home. The quality of daycare varies, so find out as much as you can about the services in advance. Children can be enrolled in pre-school at age 4 or 5, which may or may not be free. You will need to enroll children ages 6 and up in public or private school. Public schools in the U.S. are free, but as with daycare, the quality varies. Private schools are usually of higher quality, but they can be expensive.

To enroll your children in school, you will need to provide:

- Child's passport or birth certificate
- Previous school records
- Proof of immunizations

You can find out from the school what immunizations are required; the most common ones are for *measles, mumps, rubella, diphtheria* and *tetanus*.

Bank Account

Set up a bank account soon after arriving in the U.S. Look for one that has branches and ATMs near your home or school. To set up an account, most banks require the following documents:

- Passport and visa
- Second form of identification (with a photo)
- Immigration documents (I-20 or DS-2019)
- Proof of residence (A lease agreement or utility bill addressed to you at your new address can be used for this purpose.)

Arranging for Transportation

For students who live too far to walk to campus, some schools have shuttle bus services. Many large cities also have good public transportation systems. You can find schedule and route information on the transportation system's website or use a smartphone app. In some areas, transportation options are limited, and it is difficult to get around without a car.

If you decide to buy a car, do some research first by talking to other students who have bought cars and by going online. Most students choose to buy a used (pre-owned) car, and in addition to considering the price, make a decision by comparing cars':

- Year
- Make and model
- Condition
- Mileage (number of miles driven)
- Gas mileage (amount of gas used per mile)

To make an informed decision, find out all you can about a car's history; you can do this by requesting copies of all of the car's service records from the previous owner.

Getting a Driver's License

If you plan to drive, you will need to get a driver's license issued by the state you live in while in school. You will be required to take both a written and driving test. Before going to the office of the Department of Motor Vehicles (DMV), you will likely need to visit the Social Security office to obtain proof of ineligibility for a Social Security card, which is required for noncitizens getting a license in the U.S. Because state laws regarding driver's services vary (as well as office hours, testing times, etc.), check the state's DMV website before going to the office. When you go to the DMV, make sure to take your:

- Immigration documents
- Passport

- Home country driver's license (if applicable)
- Proof of residence

Keep in mind that the cost of owning a car does not end with the purchase of the vehicle. In addition paying for the car, you will have to buy a license plate and pay a registration fee every year. You will also have to pay for gas and car insurance. Insurance companies offer policies that vary in terms of price and coverage. Ask other students what companies they use and do online research to find the best policy for you. If you buy a car, you must keep proof of insurance in your car at all times.

Furnishing Your Home

Dormitories are equipped with all the necessary furnishings; students living off campus, however, need to purchase furniture and household items. Most apartments, even those that are unfurnished, have kitchen appliances, such as a refrigerator, stove/oven, and sometimes a microwave and dishwasher. For the kitchen, you may want to buy small appliances like a blender and a toaster. Also, it will be necessary to buy some basic furnishings, including: tables and chairs; a mattress, box spring, and frame; sofa; desk; and bookshelves. Some popular places to shop for low-cost furniture in the U.S. are IKEA, Target, and Wal-Mart. Some students save money by buying used furniture at places like Goodwill or online from Craigslist.

> **tip**
> If you buy an item online through websites such as Craigslist, do not go to the person's home to pick up the item. Make plans to meet the individual in a public place, such as a restaurant or coffee shop.

Whether you live on or off campus, you will need to buy some of the following household items (check any unfamiliar words in a dictionary or online):

For Cooking and Eating

aluminum foil	napkins
bottle opener	plates
bowls	pots and pans
cups/glasses	sandwich bags
cutting board	serving utensils
knives	spatula
measuring spoons, cups	utensils (forks, knives, spoons)

For Keeping Clean

cleansers	sponges
dish/dishwasher soap	toilet brush
kitchen towels	toilet paper
laundry detergent	trash bags
paper towels	trashcans

Some popular places to shop for household items are drugstores, "dollar" stores, supermarkets, thrift stores, and discount department stores.

Electrical outlets are the same in all states, and electricity is set at 110 volts and 60 cycles. Older electric plugs have two flat blades; plugs on most newer appliances also have a third round grounding pin. If you bring electrical appliances with you, you may need an adaptor to fit the outlets. You can buy small appliances at a low cost in the U.S., so it may be more convenient to buy an inexpensive appliance like a hair dryer once you arrive.

Living with Roommates

For many international students, going to school in the U.S. means living on your own for the first time, and most of you will live with one or more roommates. Living with new people is a challenge for everyone, particularly when roommates are from a different culture, and it can sometimes be frustrating and difficult. The key is to treat your roommate like you want to be treated, and to be open to new ways of doing things. Here are some other tips for getting along well with roommates:

Know yourself. Do you hate it when someone makes noise in the kitchen in the morning? Are you typically a messy person? Do you watch a lot of TV? Are you sensitive to certain odors? Think about your own habits and how they might be an issue for someone else. Let your roommate know as soon as you can about your own habits and preferences; don't wait for him/her to figure it out after being annoyed or frustrated.

Set rules and expectations at the beginning. There are many issues that must be worked out when you live with someone else, so try to come to an understanding about them at the outset.

Questions to be answered include:

- **Furnishing the home:** What furnishings (e.g., furniture, household items, appliances, decoration) will be purchased, and who will buy them? How will the costs be shared?

- **Paying the bills:** How will the bills be divided? Who will be in charge of paying the bills? What happens if a bill is not paid on time?

- **Going grocery shopping:** Will each roommate buy his or her own groceries? What about common household items such as toilet paper and trash bags? How often will shared items be bought, and by whom?

- **Cooking**: Who will do the cooking? Will you take turns? Will each person cook for himself or herself?

- **Cleaning**: How will the responsibility of house cleaning be managed? Who will clean what and how often?

- **Making noise**: How much noise (e.g., TV, music) is acceptable, and until what time at night?

- **Staying Safe:** How will you avoid fires, break-ins, or other risks to you and your property at home?

- **Respect your roommate's things.** Never borrow, use, or take anything that belongs to your roommate without asking permission first.

- **Consider how often you have guests.** You may love having your friends or your new boyfriend or girlfriend at your home, but your roommate may not. Dorm rooms and apartments get crowded very easily, and having guests often can quickly become a source of conflict.

- **Address issues early.** Is your roommate doing little things that bother you? Addressing issues when they are small is easier than dealing with them after they've become big problems.

- **Don't expect to be best friends.** Don't go into your roommate relationship thinking that you are going to be best friends. It may happen, but it may not. You should be friendly with your roommate, but also make sure to have your own social group.

Unit 2

Living in the U.S.

Part 1: Taking Care of Yourself

While living in the U.S, it is important to have fun and take care of yourself. This means sometimes cooking for yourself, and other times going out to eat, while making sure to maintain your good health and appearance. This section is intended to help you look and feel your best while in school, so that you can make the most of the experience. Here you will find information and tips on:

- Shopping for Food
- Going Out to Eat
- Shopping for Clothes
- Getting a Haircut
- Staying Healthy and Safe

Shopping for Food

One of the most challenging parts of living in a different culture is getting used to the food. Especially for students living off campus, cooking at home is a great way to be able to eat foods you are accustomed to and that you like, while also saving money. However, supermarkets (grocery stores) in the U.S. may look different and have a different selection of foods, so going shopping can sometimes be frustrating. Here are some useful words and phrases for the grocery store:

Finding things: If you are looking for something, ask an employee: *Excuse me. Could you help me? I am looking for...* or *Do you know where I can find...?*

Aisle (pronunciation: rhymes with *smile*): When you ask an employee where an item is, he or she will usually tell you the number of the aisle (row) it is on.

Paper or plastic? This is a question a cashier may ask you about the type of bag you want your groceries in. Many people choose to bring your own shopping bags as well. In some cities, there is a small charge, like five cents, if the store gives you a bag. Using your own bag is free.

To stay healthy, eat plenty of fruits and vegetables (produce). However, you may be unfamiliar with some of the produce sold in U.S. grocery stores. Here are some typical items (check any unfamiliar words in a dictionary or online):

Vegetables

asparagus
beets
broccoli
Brussels sprouts
cabbage
carrots
cauliflower
celery
corn
cucumbers
eggplant

garlic
lettuce
mushrooms
onions
peas
pepper
pumpkin
radish
spinach
squash
zucchini

Fruit

apple
apricot
avocado
bananas
blueberries
cantaloupe
cherries
coconut
grapes
lemon

lime
mango
orange
peach
pear
pineapple
plum
raisins
tomato

Going Out to Eat

One of the most popular things to do in the U.S. is going out to eat. Most cities in the U.S. offer a variety of restaurants, from fast food to fine dining. "Fast casual" is a relatively new style of restaurant, where the quality and price of food is a bit higher than at fast food places, but customers wait in line and serve themselves. Here are some terms you should understand when you go out to eat:

- **Server**: Waiter/waitress
- **Beverage**: Drink
- **Appetizer**: Small plate of food to eat before the meal
- **Entrée**: The main dish
- **Check**: The bill
- **Gratuity**: The tip
- **First available**: Taking the first available table

tip It is customary to tip the server 15 to 20%.

Here are some common questions servers ask customers:

- *How many (people in your party)?*
- *Would you like a booth?*
- *Would you like to sit at the bar?*
- *What can I get you to drink?*
- *Would you like cream or sugar?*
- *Do you need a minute (to decide)?*
- *Would you like to start with an appetizer?*
- *Will this be on the same / separate checks?*
- *Can I get you anything else?*

Here are some common questions customers ask servers:

- *Do you have any specials?*
- *What do you recommend?*
- *Does it have meat / pork / nuts in it?*
- *Can we get a highchair? (for a small child)*
- *Can I get a clean fork / spoon / knife / glass?*
- *Can we get the check please?*

Ordering Pizza

Pizza is a staple food for university students across the U.S. You can order a pizza for delivery by phone, go to a pizza place and get a pizza for "take out," or eat in the restaurant. Here are some typical pizza toppings:

anchovies	olives
artichoke hearts	pepperoni
bacon	pineapple
feta cheese	red onion
garlic	sausage
ham	spinach
green peppers	sundried tomatoes
mushrooms	

Having Coffee

Students in the U.S. often go to coffee shops (cafés) to read, study, or just hang out with friends. Because coffee shops sell much more than just regular coffee, here is some useful vocabulary to make ordering easier:

Drinks

- **cappuccino**: An Italian coffee drink made with espresso (see below)and steamed milk
- **chai tea**: Hot tea mixed with milk and spices
- **cider**: Apple juice that is usually served hot
- **decaf**: Decaffeinated coffee
- **espresso**: A strong black coffee served in a small cup, made by forcing steam through ground coffee beans.
- **frappe**: A coffee drink topped with foam made by stirring instant coffee together with a small amount of water in a shaker and adding cold water, ice cubes, and sugar
- **half and half**: A dairy product of equal parts light cream and milk
- **latte**: A coffee drink made with espresso and hot steamed milk that is milkier than a cappuccino
- **mocha**: A mixture of hot chocolate and coffee
- **skim milk**: Milk from which the cream and fat have been removed
- **smoothie**: A thick, smooth drink of fresh fruit blended with milk, yogurt, or ice cream

In addition to drinks, pastries (sweet baked goods) often sold in coffee shops. Some typical types of pastries are:

brownie	cupcake
cake	Danish
cinnamon roll	muffin
croissant	scone

Shopping for Clothes

Like going out to eat, shopping is a popular pastime in the U.S., and there are many different types of stores that sell clothing. While many high-end, expensive clothing stores can be found in malls around the country, less expensive items can be found at outlet and discount stores. Many international students enjoy shopping for bargains in the U.S. for themselves and as gifts for their families. Here are some useful words and phrases related to shopping (check any unfamiliar words in a dictionary or on-line):

- Salesclerk/salesperson
- Fitting room/dressing room
- *Excuse me. Could you help me? I am looking for...*
- *Can you tell me where the dressing rooms are?*

Clothing/Apparel

blouse	sweater
dress	tank top
pants/slacks	t-shirt
socks	tie

Accessories

belt	purse/handbag
bracelet	ring
earrings	wallet

Shoes

boots	high heels
flats	sandals
flip flops	sneakers
loafers	running shoes

Lingerie

bra

panties/underwear

pantyhose

tights

Men's Underwear

boxers

briefs

 tip

> When you enter a store, salesclerks will often ask, "Can I help you find something?" Unless you need some assistance or are looking for something in particular, you can use the common reply, "No, thank you. I'm just looking."

Outerwear

cap

coat

earmuffs

gloves

jacket

hat

raincoat

scarf

umbrella

vest

Parts of Clothing

buckle

button

collar

cuff

heel

pocket

shoestring

sleeve

sole

zipper

Getting a Haircut

Taking good care of yourself of your appearance will help you feel more comfortable while living in the U.S. One thing you will occasionally want to do to maintain your appearance is to get a haircut. In the U.S., a person who cuts both women and men's hair is a *hairstylist* or *hairdresser*; a *barber* is a person who typically cuts men's hair. When you get a haircut, some common questions you will be asked are:

- *What are we doing today?*
- *How much do you want taken off?*
- *Would you like your hair shampooed today?*
- *Do you want some (hair styling) product?*

Most hair salons require an appointment, and charge anywhere from $30 to $100. However, some places are walk-in salons (no appointment necessary) and only charge around $15 for a haircut. It is customary in the U.S. to tip the hairdresser around 15%.

Here are some phrases you can use in response:

- *I would like to make an appointment for a haircut.*
- *I need to get a haircut. Do you have any openings this week?*
- *I would like a trim. (trim = cutting off a little bit)*
- *Can you cut off two inches?*
- *Please take some off the top but not too much off the sides.*
- *I just need the bangs/beard/moustache trimmed.*

Vocabulary for hairstyles

perm (permanent wave)   moustache
bangs   part
beard   sideburn(s)

Staying Healthy and Safe

The change in environment and the stress of school can lead to mental and physical health problems, so it is important to take care of yourself. Because students are always on the go, it is tempting to skip important meals like breakfast. Likewise, it is easy to snack on sugary foods and drink caffeinated drinks in order to maintain energy, especially for late-night studying. However, these practices will actually make you feel worse in the long term. Also, keep in mind that American food is often processed and higher in salt and sugar than food in many other countries, so staying healthy in the U.S. means avoiding too many high-calorie meals. Instead, make an effort to keep healthy snacks around. Here are some more tips for staying healthy:

Get Regular Exercise

Despite your busy schedule, staying physically active is important for relieving stress, staying fit, and maintaining good health. Generally, schools in the U.S. have extensive resources to meet students' health maintenance needs – including gyms, swimming pools, and running tracks – as well as classes in yoga and other stress-relieving activities. Many students also walk or ride a bike to class to get exercise. Many schools have intramural sports teams that you can join as well.

Get Enough Sleep

As an international student, you may feel stressed by the amount of studying you have to do, and feel like the only way to do it all is to skip sleep. But in reality, you need sleep in order to pay full attention in class and to produce high-quality academic work. It is important to avoid *all-nighters* and to get a full night's rest as often as possible. Taking naps whenever you can also helps you feel refreshed.

Access Student Counseling Services

Being far away from family and friends means that you may not have the support system to help deal with all of the changes in your life. Fortunately, most schools offer free or low-cost counseling services to students. You can talk with counselors about feelings of homesickness, anxiety, and depression, as well as any personal problems you may be experiencing. Remember, feeling homesick and anxious is normal, and while accessing counseling services may feel uncomfortable at first, having someone to talk to can be very helpful when you are feeling isolated or stressed out. These services are confidential, and your privacy is secure.

Health and Hygiene

Some medications that are available over the counter in other countries require a prescription from a doctor in the U.S. You can fill a prescription at a drugstore (pharmacy). You can also purchase toiletries and other items for personal care at a drugstore, including (check any unfamiliar words in a dictionary or online):

brush

comb

cotton balls

deodorant/ antiperspirant

emery board

eye drops

fingernail clippers

fingernail polish

fingernail polish remover

floss

lotion

mouthwash

pads

powder

razor

shampoo and conditioner

shaving cream/gel

soap

suntan lotion/sunscreen

tampons

toilet paper

toothbrush

toothpaste

tweezers

Q-tips

Student Health Services

The U.S. does not have free healthcare that covers all citizens, and the cost of care can be enormous, so it is critical to have good health insurance while you are in the U.S. Many colleges and universities have student health insurance plans and, to ensure that all students are covered, participation is usually mandatory. Most schools have health clinics where students can go for primary care and referrals to other health providers.

> **tip**
>
> When you arrive on campus, find out where the student health services building is located, so you know where to go if you get sick or suffer an injury.

If you are not covered by an insurance plan offered by your school or another organization – such as a sponsoring agency – it is crucial to enroll in a plan as soon as possible. Student services staff can provide information on which plans are most often used by students.

Staying Safe

Despite what you may have seen in the movies or on the news, the U.S. is a relatively safe place to live. Stories of crime are newsworthy or entertaining precisely because they are unusual events. However, international students are often seen as potential victims by criminals, who prey on those who are new to the area and particularly vulnerable. To stay safe in the U.S., the best idea is simply to use common sense. Here are a few things to keep in mind:

Avoid walking alone or using ATMs at night, and stay away from dark or isolated streets. When you are walking, look as if you know what you are doing and where you are going; criminals like to take advantage of those who look lost, confused, or weak.

Stay alert. If you are alone, don't walk around with your head down texting or talking on the phone, as these activities keep you from being aware of your surroundings.

When you carry a purse or a bag, hold onto the strap firmly with one hand. Don't leave your bag where it is easily accessible to pickpockets. Keep your wallet in your front pocket and make sure it cannot be seen.

tip

To keep your money safe:

- Don't keep a lot of cash with you (or at home).
- If you lose your debit or credit card, report the loss immediately.
- Do not reply to emails asking for personal information or money.
- Check your bank account and credit card statements regularly.

Part 2: Interacting with Americans

Many aspects of American culture may be very different from those in your home country. These differences may cause you to feel unsure of yourself, but adjusting to a new culture is a normal process that takes time. This section is intended to help you understand Americans and their culture, and to interact with them successfully. Here you will find information and tips on:

- Understanding U.S. Culture
- Managing Culture Shock
- Meeting People
- Communicating by Email and Phone
- Interacting with Instructors

Understanding U.S. Culture

Much of what international students know about the U.S. is based on television and movies. While some ideas of American culture can be generated from these images, the United States is an immense country of over 350 million people, so there is a great deal of diversity in thought and behavior. At the same time, there are some broad cultural values that typify U.S. culture. Here are a few:

Self-Help

Americans are generally optimistic and tend to feel that we have the power to positively change our lives and the world around us. This view contributes to an ongoing desire to improve ourselves; bookstores in the U.S. are full of self-help and how-to books on everything from how to have a better marriage to how to get rich to how to improve your health. Our general outlook is that if there is a problem, there is a solution.

Competition

Personal achievement is highly prized in the United States. We are more impressed by someone who becomes successful in his or her field despite a humble background than someone who has wealth or prestige because they were born into a rich family. Americans like the idea of working hard and achieving success, and these values foster competition as well.

Change

Related to our desire to control our circumstances and improve our lives, Americans often move from city to city and state to state, and generally see change as evidence of progress. Americans focus on the future, and see new things – such as new technologies, environments, or jobs – as contributing to improvements in our lives.

Time

Life is short" and *"Time is money* are typical expressions in the U.S. Americans believe it is important to be on time, and expect others to do the same. We see time as valuable and do not like to waste our own or other people's time. Americans fill up their days with things they need or want to do (as evidenced by our reliance on agendas and schedules) and seek to accomplish as many tasks as possible in limited time. Being a multi-tasker (someone who can manage two or more tasks at one time) is valued in the U.S. because it means a person is both productive and efficient.

Equality

Equality – especially in terms of race, religion, age, sex, and gender orientation – continues to be a common goal and a shared value in the U.S. This value contributes – to the belief that anyone, no matter what their circumstances at birth, can reach their goals and achieve the American Dream. However, while equality is valued, *equity* – where everyone has access to equal opportunity, and barriers to economic and political opportunities, education, health, and basic services are eliminated – continues to be elusive in American life.

Independence

Independence is important in the U.S. Americans strive to do things themselves, and taking initiative is valued. As a student, you will be expected to do things on your own, including finding information and solving problems. That means, for example, identifying and using resources to find information you need. You may often be told to "Go to the website" or "Google it" because practically all types of information can be found online, from directions to the nearest coffee shop to answers to questions about English grammar.

Work

Children in the U.S. are often asked, *What do you want to be when you grow up?* and often the first question adults ask when they meet each other for the first time is *What do you do (for a living)?* While in other cultures people may think about their identity in other ways, such as in terms of their family background, Americans tend to define ourselves by the work that we do.

Informality

Over the last few decades, Americans have become more and more informal in the way we dress and communicate. Some of this informality, such as addressing each other by first name, is related to the desire to show equality among individuals. Also, Americans generally like to be as comfortable as possible and tend to wear more informal clothing than people in other countries. This is especially true on campus, where you will see students wearing jeans and t-shirts or – especially when the weather is warm – shorts and sandals.

Being Direct

When communicating, Americans like to get to the point. While in many cultures it is customary to begin a conversation or an email by asking about the other person's family or health, Americans will more often go straight to the topic. While this may seem rude to you, Americans see this as being efficient and respectful of your time.

Consumerism

There is some truth to the stereotype of Americans focusing on both making and spending money. Part of what drives the consumer culture is access to disposable income, as well as a desire to acquire the latest and greatest version of items – from clothes to cars to electronic devices. While in the past there was an ef fort to repair broken objects, nowadays Americans are more likely to throw something away and buy a new one.

Family Relationships

One of the most difficult aspects of American culture for many international students to understand has to do with American families. Generally speaking, Americans are not family oriented in the same way people in many other countries are. In fact, while uncles, cousins, and grandparents are considered close family members in other cultures, in the U.S. these extended family members (relatives) are not considered part of one's immediate family and may not interact with each other on a regular basis.

In the U.S., children move away from their parents' home as early as age 18, even when they are not married, which to many international students can seem that Americans do not value family relationships. However, keep in mind that, to Americans, one of the most valuable things that parents can do is teach their children to be independent and self-reliant. In fact, raising children to live on their own is a sign of successful parenting in the U.S.

In addition to values, there are some customs in the U.S. that may be different from in your country. Here are a few:

Visiting a Home

Because Americans tend to have a busy lifestyle, we usually make special arrangements for visiting friends and family, rather than just dropping by without an invitation. When you are invited to an American's home for dinner, it is polite to bring something like a bottle of wine, dessert, or flowers. When entering the home in many states, it is *not* typically expected that you will remove your shoes; however, if you invite an American to your home and would like them to remove their shoes, simply ask them politely to do so.

Tipping

People employed in service industries in the U.S. depend on tips for a large portion of their income; for this reason, they typically receive a lower wage than other workers. Therefore, it is important to leave a tip for those who provide you with a service – such as taxi drivers, restaurant servers, and hair stylists/barbers. On the bottom of a receipt, there is a space to write the amount of the tip and add that to the total you are paying. It is customary to leave a tip of 15% to 20% of the total cost.

Personal Hygiene

Different cultures have different ideas about personal hygiene; as a general rule, Americans bathe and apply deodorant every day, and brush their teeth two or more times a day. It is also common to use mouthwash to ensure fresh breath. Perfume or cologne is sometimes worn but only lightly, especially to work or school.

> In public places, there are separate restrooms (bathrooms) for men and women. All restrooms have toilets, and toilet paper should be flushed down the toilet. You are expected to wash your hands with soap and water before leaving the restroom.

Meal Times

During the week, Americans typically eat a light breakfast before going to work and have lunch around noon. Dinner, the largest meal of the day, usually begins sometime between 6 and 8 p.m. On weekends, and especially when going out to eat, Americans might eat dinner a little later, but many restaurants close around 10 or 11 p.m. every night of the week.

Arrival Times

In many countries, it is customary to arrive late to social events like dinners or weddings. This is *not* true in the U.S. If a dinner invitation gives a specific time, for example, guests are expected to arrive at that time. There is more flexibility at informal occasions like house parties; if a party is to start at 8 p.m. with no ending time, for example, it is acceptable to arrive at 8:30 or later.

Names

In the U.S., people generally have three names, in this order:

first name   middle name   last name

Example: **Victoria   Lynn   Jones**

      (first)   (middle)   (last)

First Name: This is the name people usually call you.

Middle Name: While the middle name is part of one's full name, it is not used often. Some forms will ask you to include your middle name or the initial of your middle name.

Last Name: Also known as a *surname* or *family name*, a person's last name has typically been passed down from the father, and women traditionally take last name of their husbands when they get married. However, these days some women choose to keep their last name after marriage or to "hyphenate" their last name with their husband's last name (e.g., Wilson-Jones).

Formal Terms of Address

When addressing men and women formally, the title and last name are used.

Example: Alex S. Brown = Mr. Brown

Mr. is the formal title for men, and *Miss, Mrs.* or *Ms.* are the formal titles for women. Traditionally, *Miss* is used for unmarried women and *Mrs.* for married women; however, because a woman's marriage status may be unknown, the non-specific *Ms.* is commonly used and usually preferred.

Example: Barbara Kennedy = Ms. Kennedy

The title for a man or woman with a medical or doctoral level degree is *Dr.* (doctor).

Michael Starr = Dr. Starr

Sharon Beverly Glass = Dr. Glass

U.S. Holidays

One way to enjoy your experience in the U.S. is to celebrate with Americans on their holidays. There are several holidays throughout the year; some are always on the same day, while others vary. Most schools and businesses are closed on these major holidays:

New Year's Day is celebrated on January 1, the first day of the calendar year in the U.S. Eating black eyed peas is a tradition on this day, because it is said to mean good luck for the coming year. Another American tradition is watching the Rose Bowl parade and football game in Pasadena, California, on TV.

Martin Luther King, Jr. Day became a federal holiday in 1983 and commemorates Dr. King's birthday. The holiday commemorates this civil rights hero who championed nonviolent activism. Many Americans celebrate the holiday with marches in support of peace and human rights or by doing volunteer work in their communities.

Memorial Day is a day of remembering and honoring Americans who have died while in military service. Many people visit cemeteries and memorials, and American flags are placed on graves. The holiday also marks the start of the summer vacation season.

The Fourth of July/Independence Day celebrates the country's independence from Great Britain in 1776. Americans celebrate with picnics and parades. The most popular tradition of this holiday is watching displays of colorful fireworks.

Labor Day celebrates the economic and social contributions of workers. Because it is observed on the first Monday in September, it also marks the end of the summer vacation season. To take advantage of people buying "back to school" items, Labor Day has become an important sales weekend for many stores.

Thanksgiving commemorates the meal celebrated by the Native Americans and the Pilgrims, who were the early settlers in present-day Massachusetts, to give thanks for a bountiful harvest. Families come together to eat a large meal that traditionally includes turkey and other dishes such as mashed potatoes, cranberry sauce, and pumpkin pie.

The *holiday season* occurs in December every year as Americans celebrate:

Hanukkah, an eight-day Jewish holiday commemorating the rededication of the Holy Temple in Jerusalem in the 2nd century BCE.

Christmas, a Christian holiday that celebrates the birth of Jesus Christ over 2000 years ago. The holiday is celebrated in the U.S. with a mixture of religious and secular themes and activities.

Kwanzaa, a holiday created in 1966 that honors African heritage and is observed from December 26 to January 1.

Managing Culture Shock

Living abroad can be stressful, especially where so much is unfamiliar. Many international students will at some point experience *culture shock*. Symptoms of culture shock include: an inability to concentrate, irregular eating and sleeping patterns, irritability, illness, and depression. One way to manage these emotions is to recognize that they simply reflect a stage in the process of adjustment. Although there are a variety of models of cultural adjustment, here are four that you may recognize as you make the transition to your new life:

Excitement

Sometimes called the *honeymoon period,* the first few days or weeks in a new country are often full of fun and excitement. In fact, the simple recognition that that you are finally here can be a great feeling. You have great expectations about the experiences you will have, including the knowledge and skills you will gain, the friends you will make, and the pleasure you will have seeing and doing new things. At this point, everything is new, fascinating, and exciting.

Irritation

When the excitement of arriving in a new country fades, the focus can change to differences between the home culture and the new one. You may become frustrated by the differences and feel bewildered by the new systems, rules and expectations. Especially as a student at the top of your class and accustomed to success at home, you may now feel inadequate, less productive, and unsuccessful.

Acceptance

Fortunately, over time, you will begin to adapt to the local values and customs and feel less isolated. What was strange and new is now routine and familiar. As life becomes normal, you learn to function well under the new conditions.

Confidence

Finally, you will find increased enjoyment in your new environment and an ability to function in both the old and new cultures with confidence.

Language Anxiety

Attempting to communicate effectively in a foreign language can cause discomfort and stress, sometimes known as *language anxiety*.* You may be nervous when speaking English and feel your language skills are being judged by others. Language anxiety is common and often creates a negative cycle in which anxiety about speaking means you interact little with native speakers, which further limits your ability to improve your language skills.

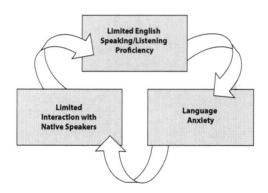

The only way to break the cycle is to make every effort to interact with native English speakers on a regular basis. Making English-speaking friends may take extra effort, but the best way to practice communicating in English is with friends in a comfortable, low-stress environment.

Learning Shock

In addition to culture shock, international students frequently experience what researchers have termed *learning shock*.** Learning shock causes feelings of confusion and uneasiness in students facing new and different ways of teaching and learning. For students from countries where learning occurs exclusively through taking and memorizing lecture notes, the interactive and communicative nature of American classrooms can cause anxiety. Some of the types of activities that are considered best practices in adult learning in the U.S. — open discussions, critical argumentation, and group work — can be challenging at first. However, you will most likely grow accustomed to these types of tasks in a short time, and begin to feel more comfortable participating actively in the classroom.

*Horwitz, E. K., Horwitz, M. B., & Cope, J. (1986). Foreign language classroom anxiety. *The Modern Language Journal, 70(2), 125-132.*

**Griffiths, D. S., Winstanley, D., & Gabriel, Y. 2005. Learning shock: The trauma of return to formal learning. *Management Learning 36(3), 275-297.*

Create New Support Systems

In your own country, you have family, friends, and institutions to support you in times of stress, depression, or anxiety. While in the U.S., it is important to find ways to get the emotional support you need as well. One way to do that is to form new relationships with those around you — roommates, neighbors, classmates, and professors. If you were part of a faith or other type of community in your country, you can also look for that kind of community in the U.S. Building this network will make you feel more at home, and your new support system can help you manage the feelings of sadness, loneliness, or frustration you may experience while in the U.S.

Participate in Social Activities

Although it sometimes takes some effort to get out of the house, sitting at home alone usually worsens the feelings of isolation or stress that come with culture shock. Joining clubs, studying in a group, and engaging in other social activities will help you to make new friends and provide you with a sense of belonging, which is key to overcoming culture shock.

Get Some R & R (Rest and Relaxation)

Think about the things you did to relax in your country. You can do these same things to help you handle stress in the U.S. Whether it is taking hot baths, going for a run, doing yoga, reading novels, watching movies, or something else, make time to do these in the U.S. You will feel more comfortable and have a sense of a normal life.

Experience Popular Culture

The more you know about what is going on around you, the more you will feel integrated into the culture and enjoy your experience in the U.S. Going to movies, watching TV shows, reading American magazines and websites — all of these activities will help you understand what is going on around you and give you things to talk to Americans about. Remember that experiencing the day-to-day popular culture of another country is one of the advantages of living abroad. Plus, if English is not your first language, doing all of these things goes a long way in improving your language skills!

Take Advantage of Opportunities

There are many things to see and do in the U.S., so take advantage of opportunities to take a break and have fun! Make a point of visiting local attractions such as parks, museums, and theaters. During school vacations, be a tourist; exploring new places is a great way to relax and clear your mind of homework and tests

Be Patient

The most important thing is to remember that adaptation is a process that takes time. Studying in the U.S. is an important and valuable investment, and while it may be quite a challenge now, there will be a big payoff in your future.

Challenges for Families

Although living and studying in the U.S. can often be challenging for international students, it can be equally difficult for students' families. While you are busy in classes, meetings, and other activities during the day, your spouse may spend much of his or her time at home, resulting in feelings of isolation, loneliness, and homesickness. This is especially true for spouses who lack transportation and/or who have limited English skills. Some of the ways your spouse can address these issue are to:

• Enroll in English classes to improve their language skills

• Participate in programs and activities for spouses, sponsored by the school or local organizations

• Take classes in their areas of interest, like art, music, or cooking

• Get involved with a local religious or cultural organization

• Form a social network with other spouses

Meeting People

One of the benefits of studying in the U.S. is the chance to interact with people you would not otherwise have an opportunity to meet. As you begin to interact with Americans, most likely you will find them open and friendly. At the same time, in the U.S., as in every culture, there are unwritten rules about how to interact with others. Knowing the American cultural norms around communication will facilitate good communication in the U.S. Here are a few:

Introductions

When meeting someone for the first time, both men and women firmly shake hands. The most common phrase to use when meeting someone for the first time is, *Nice to meet you.* The appropriate response is, *Nice to meet you, too.* As you meet people, you will find yourself in the position of introducing people you know to each other. When you do, it is a good idea to provide some information about each person. Here are a couple of examples:

Kate, this is my friend Yu. She's from China. She's a first-year student at the business school. Yu, this is Kate. She's getting a Ph.D. in chemistry.

Felong, this is Dr. Siler, my history professor. Dr. Siler, this is my roommate, Felong. He's from South Korea.

Greetings

There are a few common questions that Americans ask on a daily basis as a polite greeting when seeing others in passing. Here are some examples:

- *How are you?*
- *How are you doing?* (Often sounds like *Howyadoin'?*)
- *How's it going?*
- *How have you been?*

The best reply is: *Fine* or *Good*; and then, *How are you?* Or *How are you doing?*

When someone greets you in this way, it is not necessary to stop and talk unless the person indicates he or she has time to chat. If you would like to stop and chat with someone you greet, you can say, *Do you have a minute to talk?*

> **tip**
>
> While in many countries you are expected to greet everyone individually upon entering a room, in the U.S. this is often seen as disruptive. Especially if you arrive late, it is best to be as quiet as possible when entering a meeting or class.

Getting to Know Americans

You can get to know American students by chatting in class and by going out to eat or for coffee. While you are together, you can start by making *small talk*. Small talk is very general, light conversation. Some common topics in the U.S. are:

- news/current events
- sports
- movies and TV shows
- music/concerts
- travel
- shopping/clothes
- cooking/restaurants
- celebrity gossip

Americans also engage in a variety of pastimes, and one way to get to know them is to talk with them about those activities, especially if it is an interest you share. Some typical activities Americans enjoy are: photography, art, reading, camping, playing a musical instrument, and singing. Many Americans also like to engage in physical activities such as hiking, jogging, biking, swimming, water skiing, snow skiing, playing sports, or working out at a gym.

Another good way to engage an American in conversation is to ask questions. Some common conversation starters are:

- *Do you live on campus/off-campus? Do you like your dorm/apartment complex?*
- *I like those (shoes/sunglasses/earrings). Where did you get them?*
- *Are there any good places to eat around here?*
- *Have you been to (restaurant/mall)? Did you like it?*
- *What do you think about this class?*
- *How do you get to school every day? Does it take long?*

Some international students are concerned that they may ask an American a question or make a comment that will be offensive, as they have been told that Americans are sensitive about many subjects. In fact, most Americans are fairly open to talking about a range of subjects. The only questions that are generally considered inappropriate to discuss with someone you don't know well are about race, religion, and politics. In addition, Americans tend not to talk about money (particularly salaries) even with their close friends. It is also rude to make comments or ask questions about a person's height or weight.

> **tip**
>
> While Americans tend to be direct in communications, it is also true we make an effort to avoid being offensive by, for example, making negative comments about someone's appearance. The general rule is, "If you can't say something nice (to or about someone), don't say anything at all."

One of the best ways to meet Americans is to get involved in extracurricular activities – those activities that take place within the university community but outside the classroom. Examples include holding a student government office, participating in student club activities, and playing on a sports team.

Doing volunteer work is a great way to meet people, practice your English, and get involved in the community. It's also an excellent way to gain practical experience. Volunteer activities can include anything from cleaning up a hiking trail to teaching children to read to visiting senior citizens in a nursing home. If you do volunteer work, keep a record of the information for your résumé. Specifically, make note of the organization you worked for, the dates you worked, and the type of work you did. The career center at your college or university can help you find volunteer opportunities.

> **tip**
>
> Invitations often include the phrase "RSVP," which stands for a French phrase that means "Respond please." When you see RSVP on an invitation, it means you are expected to contact the hosts of the event to let them know whether you will be attending. To be respectful to the host, it is very important to respond (to RSVP) to all events when requested.

Making Friends

Newcomers to the U.S. often find Americans to be open and friendly, and are surprised to see how often we smile at and even greet people we don't know. At the same time, international students sometimes confuse being *friendly* with being *friends*. Being friendly is simply a personal characteristic; being friends means developing a close relationship over time. Because Americans value privacy and are cautious about making commitments, it often takes time to move beyond superficial relationships into real friendships. In addition, there are other reasons that may explain why it is sometimes hard to get to know Americans:

They may not know what to talk about. Many Americans, especially those who have not traveled abroad, may be hesitant to initiate conversation because they don't know anything about your country or your culture. They may not know what to say or what questions to ask. Instead of revealing their lack of knowledge, or risking saying something that might sound silly or offensive, they play it safe and choose not to say anything.

They may not know you are interested in meeting them. The United States comprises a diverse population, and many schools are located in large urban areas that are home to people from all around the world. Therefore, as an international student, you might not stand out as someone who is new to the U.S. On campus, American students might not recognize that you are an international student; or, if they do, may assume that you already have your own group of friends that you would prefer to spend time with. American students who have never lived abroad might not realize that living in the U.S. can be challenging for international students and that it would be a good idea to reach out to you in friendship.

They may be shy. No matter where you go, you will find that some people are more outgoing, friendly, and interested in meeting new people than others. In order to make friends with American students, look for those who seem particularly sociable and extroverted.

They may be *really* busy. American students are almost always doing something; they may be studying for a test, doing homework, researching a paper, or looking for a job. The fact is that Americans students are generally very busy — just like international students! Although they may not have some of the challenges that international students face, they could have family obligations, part-time or full-time jobs, or other extracurricular activities that keep their free time to a minimum. This is life in a university environment, and unfortunately, it makes it more difficult to form friendships with American students. Just remember, in this case, that you are all in the same boat!

While in many countries, family and friends maintain daily contact with each other, this is less common in the U.S. Some time might pass without any interaction even between friends. When they do spend time together, Americans generally schedule that time in advance, much as they do other activities.

Using Common Expressions

Most of your day-to-day conversations at school with faculty, staff, and other students will be informal. Here are a few common expressions for informal communications in a school setting:

Be right back (to go and return immediately)

Can you stay here while I go get my book? I'll be right back.

Catch up (do tasks that were not done at the original time)

I didn't do my homework for a week. Now I have to catch up.

Catch on (understand)

At first I didn't understand the assignment, but now I am starting to catch on.

Check it out (investigate)

I think that movie got good reviews. I'll have to go online and check it out.

Fill (one) *in* (provide missing information to someone)

I missed the meeting this morning. Can you fill me in?

Find out (discover information)

I'd better find out what time the class starts, or I may be late.

Get back to (communicate with someone at a later time)

I'm afraid I don't know where the orientation meeting is. I'll ask my roommate and get back to you as soon as I can.

Go over (review)

Can we go over the instructions again? Maybe this time it will be clearer.

Hold on (wait)

Hold on. I need to get my jacket before we leave the house.

The classroom is always very cold.

In time (by the deadline)

If you don't leave now, you won't get to the presentation in time!

Let (one) **know** (give information)

She said she would let us know as soon as the grades are posted.

Look into it (investigate something)

I didn't know about the new class being offered. I'll look into it and see if I can register for it.

Make it (attend)

If I don't have class this afternoon, I should be able to make it to the workshop.

Make up (do uncompleted work)

I have to make up some assignments because I was out of town for three days.

Move up/back (change the time)

Can we move our meeting up to three p.m. so I can leave early?

On time (punctual)

If the shuttle is on time, it should be here in five minutes.

Stop by (visit for a short time)

The professor told me to stop by her office at 2:00.

Turn in (submit)

We had to turn in our papers even if we weren't finished.

Using Appropriate Language

Beyond "please" and "thank you," there are other phrases you can use to be courteous in your interactions with others. Use the following introductory phrases to be polite when speaking:

I'm afraid that...

I'm afraid that I can't sign up to volunteer yet because I won't know my schedule until next week.

I'm afraid that I have to leave early. I have a doctor's appointment this afternoon.

It would be great if you/we could...

It would be great if you could send me that file.

It would be great if we could meet early next week.

Would you mind...?

Would you mind explaining that problem again?

Would you mind if we changed the meeting time to 3 p.m.?

Would it be possible to...?

Would it be possible to go at 2:00 instead of at 3:00?

Would it be possible to get a copy of the syllabus for the class?

Describing People

These terms are appropriate for describing people in English:

Age: Avoid using the words *old* or *elderly* when describing a person. The terms *senior* or *older adult* are preferred.

Race: The terms *African American* and *Black* are used interchangeably, though *African American* is generally considered the preferred term. The terms *Hispanic* and *Latino*(or *Latina* for a woman) are also often used interchangeably, though *Lati-*

no/Latina are generally considered the preferred terms. *White* and *Asian* are also acceptable terms for describing race.

> **tip**
>
> The term *Native American* refers to a member of a group of people who are indigenous to North America, also known as *American Indians*. Although the term *American* can refer to natives of North, Central, and South American countries, there is no specific term in English for someone from the U.S. Therefore, when referring to someone who is a citizen of the United States, we often use the term *American*.

Sexual Orientation/Gender Identity: A homosexual man is generally referred to as a *gay* man, while a homosexual woman is a *lesbian*. Other commonly used terms are *bisexual* man/woman and *transgender*. LGBTQ is a common acronym that stands for lesbian, gay, bisexual, transgender, and queer (or questioning), and recognizes the diversity of sexuality and gender identities.

Religion: The U.S. is home to followers of all of the world's major religions. Here are the names of the some of the most common religions practiced in the U.S. and the terms for their adherents:

Religion	Person
Christianity	Christian
Judaism	Jew
Islam	Muslim
Buddhism	Buddhist
Hinduism	Hindu

British and American English

Many international students have studied British English (also known as the Queen's English), which can cause some confusion in the U.S. Here are some examples of words that are different in British and American English:

British English	American English
autumn	fall/autumn
barrister/solicitor	attorney/lawyer
bathing costume	bathing suit/swimsuit
biscuit	cookie
(restaurant) bill	bill/check
bonnet (car)	hood
boot (car)	trunk
car park	parking lot
chemist's shop	drugstore/pharmacy
cinema	movies
cooker	stove
crisps	potato chips/chips
chips	French fries
city centre	downtown
cupboard	closet
dustbin/rubbish bin	garbage can/trashcan
engaged (telephone)	busy
film	movie/film

garden	yard/lawn
ground floor	first floor/ground floor
handbag	purse/handbag
hire (car)	rent
holiday	vacation
hoover	vacuum cleaner
jumper	sweater
lift	elevator
lorry	truck
mad	crazy/insane
mobile	cell phone/mobile phone
mum	mom
maths	math
motorbike	motorcycle
notice board	bulletin board
pants/underpants	underwear
pavement	sidewalk
petrol	gas/gasoline
post	mail
postbox	mailbox
postcode	zip code
pub	bar
public toilet	public bathroom/restroom

queue	line
railway	railroad
rubber	eraser
rubbish	garbage/trash
rucksack	backpack
shop	store/shop
surname	last name
sweets	candy
tap	faucet
torch	flashlight
telly	TV
timetable	schedule
trousers	pants/slacks
tube/underground	subway
wardrobe	closet
WC	bathroom/restroom
zip	zipper

Communicating by Email and Phone

One of the most surprising aspects of life in the U.S. for many international students is the frequent use of email for communication. While in other countries it is more common to communicate face-to-face or by phone, email has become the primary form of communication to students from faculty, staff, and administration, in the U.S., and students are expected to read and respond to emails every day. It is important to use correct spelling and punctuation in emails. Informal abbreviations and words like *wanna* (for "want to") are not appropriate in emails to school staff or faculty.

tip If your native language is written from right to left, make sure that when you send emails in English the writing is from left to right.

Because you will receive a great deal of email while you are in the U.S., you might be tempted to ignore or simply delete messages. However, you will be receiving emails with important information from a variety of sources, including school faculty and staff, academic advisors, and your school's office of international student and scholarship services. You may also receive emails from U.S. immigration services and other government offices, and from businesses such as your bank or credit card company, as well as from potential employers. Therefore, read all emails and promptly follow instructions or take any action requested; otherwise, you may miss critical information and deadlines.

Writing Emails

There are a few common phrases you can use when communicating by email with friends, classmates, professors, and others.

Greetings

- Dear Dr. Chu,
- Good morning Ms. Livingston,

• Hey Nikki,

Getting Started

- How are you doing?
- I hope you are doing well.
- I hope you had a nice weekend.
- I hope you enjoyed the holidays.
- I enjoyed your lecture this morning on...
- Thank you for your help with...

Scheduling an Appointment

- Are you free on Monday at 10 a.m. to meet about...?
- Do you have any time on Thursday?
- Are you available this week to talk about...?
- Are you free for lunch/coffee?
- Would you like to have lunch on Wednesday?
- What time would you like to meet?
- What day/time works for you?
- Does that work for you?
- I am available after 2 p.m. on Thursday.
- I will be out of town this week, but would be happy to meet next week.
- I will let you know ASAP (as soon as possible).
- Sounds good!
- That works for me.

Making Requests

- Would you have time in the next week or so to look over my paper?
- Could you forward that email to me?

Closing

- Thank you!
- Thanks so much for your help!

(tip)

> When you use a word like "today" or "tomorrow'"
> in an email, to avoid confusion it is useful to spec-
> ify the day you are referring to, as the receiver
> may not read the email the same day that you
> send it. For example, "Can we meet tomorrow
> (Thursday) at 11 a.m.?"

Communicating by Phone

When calling someone on the phone, it is important to know these key phrases to use:

When the person you are calling answers the phone, say:

Hi. This is (your name). *May I speak to* (name)?

When the person you want to speak to answers, begin by saying:

Hi. This is (your name). *How are you?*

If the person you are calling does not answer, leave a message with your name, telephone number, and reason for calling. Speak slowly and spell words when necessary. Give the person at least 24 hours before you try calling again; students, staff, and faculty are generally very busy and may not be able to return your call immediately.

When writing your telephone number, write it in the format traditionally used in the US: (area code) three digits – four digits

Example: (202) 555-5555

Listening Skills

Becoming accustomed to the way Americans speak takes time, and at first it may be difficult to participate in conversations with native speakers, especially during classroom/group activities. Finding opportunities to practice listening outside of class can help. Here are some resources for practice:

Radio:

National Public Radio: http://www.npr.org

Videos:

Ted Talks: http://www.ted.com

YouTube: http://www.youtube.comNational News

Websites:

http://www.CBSnews.com

http://www.MSNBC.msn.com

http://www.ABCnews.go.com

http://www.CNN.com

Movies/TV Series. Watching movies and TV series is a great way to practice listening, especially because it provides the opportunity to hear a variety of people in natural conversation.

Interacting with Instructors

Professor-student relationships are generally less formal in the U.S. than in other countries. Professors are often friendly and interact with students outside of class. Despite this general environment of informality, however, it is customary to address professors using their title and last name (e.g., *Dr. Black*) unless they ask to be called by their first name. Likewise, except during regularly scheduled office hours, if you want to meet with a professor, you are expected to make an appointment for a meeting in advance, usually by email.

> Some students find it helpful to record professors' lectures and listen to them again after class. If you would like to do this, simply ask your instructor for permission to record the class.

Although it may be intimidating at first, establishing good relationships with your professors and teaching assistant (TAs) is one of the best ways to be successful in school. They are a great source of academic support and may be some of the most important contacts you make. To make a good impression on your professors, make sure to always:

- Arrive for class on time
- Sit near the front of the room
- Pay attention
- Participate actively

If you encounter a problem in class or with an assignment, talk to the instructor as soon as possible. Professors and TAs are usually very willing to help, but won't know there is an issue unless you communicate with them. If you are going to be absent from a class, let the instructor know ahead of time. Keep in mind that you are always responsible for information and materials provided in class, even when you are absent.

tip

TAs (Teaching Assistants; also called GAs or Graduate Assistants at some institutions) are students who assist professors with instructional responsibilities; it is a good idea to get to know your T.A.s, as they are great resources for answering questions about the class and providing guidance on assignments.

It is important not to engage in other activities during class time, such as texting or checking Facebook, because instructors are aware when this occurs and it shows that you are not fully engaged in the class. Remember, just as you notice the behaviors of your instructors, your instructors observe your behavior as well, and it influences their impression of you. Showing respect and interest can make a difference, especially when it is time to ask for assistance in the form of recommendation letters, research positions, and job contacts!

While in some countries it is considered disrespectful to look a person of authority in the eye, the opposite is true in the U.S. When talking with Americans, it is important to look them in the eye to show that you are listening.

Unit 3

Being a Successful Student

Part 1: Meeting Expectations

The workload for both undergraduate and graduate students in the U.S. is heavy, and the expectations you must meet to be a successful student may be different from what you are accustomed. For example, in the U.S., doing well academically requires more than memorizing information and taking tests; students are often required to work on projects and participate in class discussions. This section looks at some of the important expectations of students in and outside the classroom. Here you will find information and tips on:

- Following the Honor and Conduct Codes
- Meeting Deadlines
- Doing the Reading
- Participating in Class
- Making Presentations

Following the Honor and Conduct Codes

Schools in the U.S. have honor and conduct codes to ensure personal responsibility and professional standards. Some of these rules may be new and unfamiliar to you; nonetheless, you are required to follow them. It is your responsibility to become familiar with your university's codes and to ask staff or professors if any anything is unclear. Ignorance or misunderstanding of the rules is not considered an excuse for breaking them.

Honor Code

Violations of an academic honor code usually include any action by a student demonstrating dishonesty or a lack of academic integrity. Here are a few examples:

- **Cheating:** Seeking, receiving, or giving information about the content of an examination prior to its release or during its administration
- **Plagiarizing:** Presenting as one's own work the expression, words, or ideas of another person
- **Falsifying research data**: Creating information not actually collected, or altering information or data
- **Forging academic documents:** Writing a school official's signature on an academic document
- **Engaging in sexual harassment or assault:** Engaging in verbal or physical conduct with someone without his or her consent

tip

When you go to take an exam, bring everything you need so you don't have to ask other students to lend you an item such as a pen or a calculator. Talking to another student is prohibited during tests and may be considered cheating.

Conduct Code

Typical violations of a conduct code include:

- Physically harming or threatening to harm another person
- Sexual misconduct or abuse, such as sexual assault, rape, or other forms of nonconsensual sexual activity
- Illegally possessing, using, distributing, manufacturing, selling, or being under the influence of alcohol or other drugs
- Engaging in harassment, which is behavior that is sufficiently severe or pervasive that it threatens an individual or substantially interferes with his or her employment, education, or access to school programs or activities
- Stealing, vandalizing, damaging, destroying, or defacing school property or the property of others

Response to Violations

Different schools have different protocols for responding to cases of honor code violations, but the process usually involves the student going before a committee that determines whether a violation was committed. If a student is found guilty of an honor code violation, the consequences range from receiving a failing grade on an assignment to failing a course to expulsion

from school. In the case of sexual or other types of harassment, the school may contact local law enforcement authorities as well.

Avoiding Plagiarism

One of the most common violations of a school's honor code is plagiarism. Plagiarism is a serious issue because in the U.S. a person's work – including writing, art, music, and design – is considered his or her *intellectual property* and cannot be used without permission or credit. Because plagiarism is often a new and confusing topic for international students, it is important to learn what it is and how to avoid it. Some clear examples of plagiarism are:

- Buying, stealing, copying or borrowing a paper (including copying an entire paper or article from the Internet)
- Having someone else write a paper for you
- Copying sections of a text from a source without using quotation marks and proper citation

To avoid plagiarism, track your sources as you research, and when you write, give credit for anything you obtained from another person, including:

- Words or ideas presented in a magazine, book, newspaper, song, TV program, movie, web page, computer program, letter, advertisement or any other medium
- Information from interviewing or conversing with another person, face to face, over the phone or in writing
- Another's exact words or unique phrase
- A reprint of any diagrams, illustrations, charts, pictures, or other visual material
- Reuse or repost of any electronically available media, including images, audio, video, or other media

Quoting Sources

A direct quotation (quote) is a word-for-word reproduction of a source's writing or speech. Only use direct quotes for language that is particularly expressive or relevant; too many direct quotes can give the impression that you have not thoroughly read and understood the source material yourself, but are simply repeating what someone else has said. Generally, it is better to include only quotations of words or short phrases from a source, instead of entire sentences or paragraphs.

When you choose to use a direct quotation, remember to:

- Keep the source author's name in the same sentence as the quote (e.g., Martin Luther King Jr. said, "I have a dream.")
- Put the quoted material inside quotation marks
- Use ellipsis points (...) to indicate any omitted text

Paraphrasing

In addition to using quotation marks to indicate direct quotes from a source, the best way to avoid plagiarism is to paraphrase well. Paraphrasing means synthesizing the information and expressing it in your own words (and using proper citation). Effective paraphrasing makes your writing more concise, strengthens your argument, and distinguishes your original ideas from those of others. Paraphrasing source material effectively involves three steps:

- Deciding what original source material to paraphrase
- Summarizing the source information using your own words and sentence structure
- Using attribution phrases such as, "According to..." and "The authors note that..." to introduce paraphrased material

Students are often confused about what is and what is not paraphrasing. Paraphrasing is NOT copying the original material and then simply replacing a few words with synonyms or rearranging the words. Paraphrasing means expressing the information, ideas, and meaning of the original source accurately, using your own words and structure.

Here are a couple of examples:

Original Text

The primary strength of the social ecological model is that it draws on what we have learned from sociology, psychology and related fields about human behavior and the complexity of the influences on people's beliefs, attitudes and actions. The framework recognizes that an individual's health behavior is not a result of a singular influence, but on a number of different factors. Complex problems require complex solutions, and employing this broad approach encourages the utilization of a combination of efforts targeting various levels of impact on health. Moreover, this comprehensive approach is more likely to sustain prevention efforts over time than a singularly focused intervention. By addressing the influences on health behavior at the individual, interpersonal, organizational, community and policy levels, the social ecological framework views issues from a number of perspectives, greatly increasing the impact on individuals, who are ultimately responsible for making and maintaining the lifestyle changes necessary to reduce risk and improve health.

Paraphrase

The social ecological model, because it addresses health from the individual, interpersonal, organizational, community and policy levels, has a greater impact than models that take a narrow, one-dimensional view of the influences on health behaviors (Patrick, 2013).

Original Text

Nonfatal intentional injuries in adolescent girls – such as cuts, bruises, and damage to internal organs – result from deliberate self-harming behaviors that most often include skin-cutting, burning, scratching, banging or hitting body parts, hair-pulling and the ingestion of toxic substances. Research suggests that the incidence of self-harm is increasing in teen populations, and that girls are more likely to engage in these harmful behaviors than boys. Adolescents often engage in self-harm in an effort to reduce acute psychological pain and emotional distress associated with a number of different factors, including: physical, sexual or psychological abuse and psychological disorders, including anxiety and depression.

Paraphrase

As a response to emotional distress, self-harm behaviors – including cutting, hair-pulling, and ingesting toxic substances – are a growing health problem among teenage girl (Patrick, 2013).

Note how in both examples, the paraphrased version expresses the information from the original source in a concise and accurate way, while using the student's own words and structure. Also, both examples give credit to the original author through a citation.

Meeting Deadlines

As a student, you will have many classes and assignments to manage, and getting assignments done on time is critical to your success. Remember, it is your responsibility to regularly check the syllabus for each class, turn homework in on time, and be ready for exams.

International students sometimes confuse the words **due** and **deadline**. **Due** is an adjective. (*When is the paper* **due***? It is* **due** *on Wednesday*.) **Deadline** is a noun.*I have many deadlines to meet this week in my European history class. The first* **deadline** *is Tuesday.*

To avoid missing deadlines, it is important to manage your time effectively. At the beginning of each term, look though all of your syllabi/assignment lists, and put each assignment and test on your calendar. You can use a paper calendar or download an app or an electronic one. Then, at the beginning of each week, look at what assignments are due that week and make a schedule for completing them. Remember to schedule blocks of time each day to study. Here are some additional tips for staying on track:

Prioritize your Assignments

When you sit down to study, begin with the most difficult subject. You'll be fresh, and have more energy to tackle the most challenging tasks.

Avoid Procrastination

Procrastination means putting off for later tasks that need to be done today. Procrastinating only adds to stress, so begin assignments as early as possible. Then, if you have questions or have to edit or redo something, you will have time before the assignment is due.

tip

Although every course is different, there is a general rule in the U.S. that one hour of class time requires two to three hours of study outside of class. The amount of time may even be more for international students.

Using Free Time Wisely

When you have short periods of time – while riding the bus to campus, for example – take advantage of the opportunity to do things like review your notes or complete short reading assignments.

Reviewing Information

Reviewing class information just before class will refresh your memory and help put new information in context. Likewise, reviewing your notes immediately after class helps you put the information in your long-term memory.

Because there are many subjects of interest, international students sometimes take more courses than they can handle. To ensure time for study and other activities, create a class schedule that is manageable for you.

Doing the Reading

One of the biggest challenges for students is managing the large amount of reading required for your courses. Depending on your discipline, the number of pages you have to read every day can number in the hundreds. The reading workload is especially an issue for students reading in a second language. Here are a couple of tips for managing the reading workload:

Look at the class assignment before you begin reading. Ask yourself: "What will I be asked to do with the information in the reading?"

For example:

Will I be asked to...

- get a general overview of a topic?
- answer specific questions?
- discuss the information in a small group?
- write about my opinion on an issue presented in the reading?
- write a paper describing the pros and cons of an issue discussed in the readings?
- synthesize information from several readings in a paper?

When you have determined what you will be asked to do with the information in the readings, let that guide the way you read the material. For example:

- If you are going to present your opinion in writing, think about and note your own views about the information while you read.
- If you just need to get the general idea, focus on reading any summary or abstract that may be provided or skim the materials for the main topics.
- If you will be answering a list of questions, scan for the information that provides the answers.

Take notes and highlight information as you read. Taking notes is a great way to keep focused, especially when you are feeling sleepy or having trouble concentrating. Highlighting key words, phrases, and sentences also helps you to go back and find relevant information when you need it for your assignment.

Skimming and Scanning

Skimming and scanning are techniques can be used when time is limited and you have a lot of material to read. Skimming is used to get the general idea from the materials. You can usually get the main idea of a text by reading:

- The first sentence of each paragraph
- The first and last paragraphs of the document
- The title, headings, and subheadings

Scanning is used to find particular pieces of information. Use headings and subheadings, the table of contents, and/or the index to help you locate the specific information you are looking for.

Participating in Class

Participating in class and small groups is an integral part of higher education in the U.S. In fact, in some classes, a percentage of your grade may be based on participation.

Participation in class includes asking and answering questions, making comments, and giving your opinion. Active participation is encouraged in American classrooms because sharing information and ideas is seen as a way for students to deepen their understanding of what they are learning, and to learn not only from the teacher and textbooks but from each other. In addition, student participation helps instructors know whether the students understand what is being taught or if further explanation or help is needed. Here are some tips for effectively participating in class:

Be Prepared

Do the reading early so you have time to think about and understand what you read before class. While reading, think about the ideas critically and note any points about which you have opinions. Think about how you would express these ideas in class. Make a note of anything you are not clear about and prepare a question to ask in class to clarify your understanding.

Sit in the Front of the Class

It is easier to see, hear, and get the professor's attention when you have a question or comment if you are sitting up front, and you are also more likely to stay focused on the instructor's lecture. Likewise, professors are more likely to notice you if they see you in class regularly, which can help as you establish a good relationship.

Interact with Other Students

Make a conscious effort to get to know other students in the class. It is much less intimidating to speak in front of people you know than in front of an audience of strangers.

Ask Questions

Classroom discussion is not all about showing what you know. Asking questions of the instructor and other students demonstrates your interest in the subject and is a valuable way of participating. By asking questions from the reading material, you can demonstrate your interest in the topic and indicate to the instructor that you have done the required reading. Keep in mind that there is not always one "right" answer; rather, there is an expectation that a range of ideas will be discussed, and that they will be supported with reasons and evidence.

Taking Notes in Class

Taking good lecture notes encourages you to listen carefully and helps you remember key information. You do not have to write down everything; note the main points using key words or short sentences. Instructors usually give clues to what students need to remember by writing material on the board, repeating information, and using phrases like "There are two points of view on…" and "The third reason is…"

Build on What Other Classmates Say

If you can, link to what has already been said by emphasizing, agreeing, or disagreeing with a previous speaker. However, when agreeing, you don't want to simply repeat word for word what a previous speaker said; you want to add something about your own experience or viewpoint. You can use phrases like *That was a really good point* or *I agree with you about…*When you are disagreeing, you don't want to be rude; again, simply share how your own experience or viewpoint is different. You can use phrases like: *I think you made an interesting point about that, but my experience has been different. I have found that…* A common pattern is to partially agree or acknowledge the other person's point before you disagree: *I see what you're saying, but as I see it, …* or *That's a good point; however, ….*

Expect to Feel a Little Nervous

Practically everyone feels nervous speaking in public — particularly in a foreign language. Some students worry about making errors; they don't want to express their ideas unless they can do so without making mistakes. But the truth is that the instructor and other students are much more interested in *what* you have to say than *how* you say it. Also, practice helps; the more you participate, the more comfortable you will feel speaking up.

Group Work

In addition to engaging in class discussions, participating in class often means working on projects or papers with other students in small groups. Instructors in the U.S. often have students work in small groups when a project that is too large or complex for an individual, or to give students the opportunity to share information and points of view on a topic. In addition, group work is considered a valuable method of instruction because students:

- work on common goals with others from different backgrounds, experience, and skills, and consider alternative points of view or solutions to a problem
- participate more actively than in a large classroom setting
- strengthen interpersonal communication and teamwork skills

Group work is often particularly challenging for international students, who are unaccustomed to collaborating on academic work and who find it hard to keep up with conversations in groups of native English speakers. Here are some tips for working in groups:

- Always do your share. If you are concerned that you can't contribute as much as other students because of lack of experience or limited writing skills, then volunteer to take on more than your share of other tasks that you can do well.

- If you have a hard time following the group conversation, let the other students know that you want to understand everything, and that is helpful when they speak more slowly. Ask for clarification of particular words or points that you don't understand.

- Be respectful of everyone's time. Come to meetings on time and meet all deadlines. When you are meeting with your group, stay focused on the task so that you do not waste time.

- Working with other students on a project can be stressful and present unique challenges, but it is important to stay positive throughout. Do your part to stay on track, make progress, and keep the environment friendly and comfortable.

Giving Presentations

In addition to gaining knowledge in a particular academic discipline, in the U.S. education system it is considered important that students learn how to communicate that knowledge effectively with others. Students are often required to develop and deliver presentations in class. Generally, students create slides and speak from notes. Here are some tips for designing presentation slides:

- Use at least a 24-point font size and an even larger font (35-45 points) for titles.
- Avoid having more than six lines of text per slide.
- Use dark text on a light background or light text on a dark background.
- Use graphics that are appropriate for your audience and related to the topic of the slide.
- Use the same style of graphics throughout the presentation (e.g., all color photographs).

When creating slides, remember to capitalize the first letter of each word of a title (except prepositions and articles). Also, be consistent; if you have information in bullet points, for example, start each statement with the same type of word (e.g., noun, verb). Here is an example:

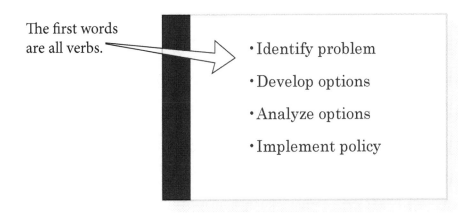

The first words are all verbs.

- Identify problem
- Develop options
- Analyze options
- Implement policy

Before you finish creating your presentation, check your spelling and grammar, as mistakes are easily noticed up on a screen. Practice your presentation several times so that it goes smoothly. You can make notecards to refer to, but don't just read your entire presentation. Here are a few phrases you can use:

Introduction

> *To begin, let's look at...*
>
> *First, I would like to talk about...*
>
> *Let me give you some background on...*

Explanation

> *As you can see...*
>
> *You can see here that...*
>
> *This slide shows that...*
>
> *The main point here is that...*

Transition

> *In a moment I will talk about...*
>
> *Now let's look at...*
>
> *The next thing I want to talk about is...*

Conclusion

> *In conclusion...*
>
> *So, what I hope you will remember from this presentation is...*

Delivery

The success of your presentation depends a great deal on how you well deliver it. Here are some tips:

- Keep your head up and make eye contact with people in all parts of the room.
- If you can, come out from behind the lectern.
- Smile and use a tone of voice that shows you are enthusiastic about your topic.
- Talk at a normal pace (not too fast or too slow).
- If someone asks a question, repeat the question so that everyone can hear it before you answer.

Part 2: Writing Papers

In addition to sharing information and ideas through class discussions and group projects, students are expected to demonstrate their understanding of course content through writing essays and research papers. Developing the ability to write well – clearly conveying complex ideas in a well-structured, concise format – is, in fact, a primary goal of education, to prepare students for careers in a wide variety of fields. This section looks at ways to strengthen your academic writing skills. Here you will find information and tips on:

- Preparing to Write
- Doing Research
- Citing Sources
- Choosing the Right Words
- Using Effective Writing Practices
- Editing Your Paper

Preparing to Write

Before you begin writing, there are a few things you can do to ensure that your paper meets your instructor's requirements and represents your best effort. First, read the instructions carefully – several times if necessary – to make sure make sure you understand what to do. Failure to follow instructions can have hurt your grade; if you have any questions, ask your professor or teaching assistant for clarification.

Once you are clear on the instructions, create an outline of your document. An outline will help you make sure your ideas are well organized and flow logically from one to another. Your outline should include the main points and details to support each point.

Formatting

Instructors often specify the formatting for a paper, including font type and size, line spacing, and margin size. If no particular formatting is specified, it is a recommended to use the following formatting:

> **Type Size**: 12 pt. type
>
> **Font Style**: Times New Roman
>
> **Margins**: 1-inch margins
>
> **Line Spacing**: Double-spaced

However, it's best to ask your professor about formatting requirements if you have not been told.

Put your name and the page number on every page. You can do this in the header (top of the page)or footer (bottom of the page). If you have titles or headings, capitalize the first letter of all words (except articles and prepositions).

tip

Traditionally, writers used one space between words and two spaces between sentences. Nowadays, it is more common to use one space in both cases.

Purpose

The purpose of each academic paper guides the organization and development of the paper. The assignment instructions often provide words and phrases that indicate the purpose of the paper, such as:

Compare and Contrast: Identify similarities (comparing) and differences (contrasting)

Evaluate: Make judgments to determine the value of something

Critically Consider: Identify strengths and weaknesses

Analyze: Identify and evaluate components of an idea or theory and their contribution to a whole

Argue: Defend a position using evidence

Explain: Give a step-by-step description of an idea, concept or theory

Once you have identified the purpose of the document, you can think about how to organize the information in the body of the paper. Here are some examples:

Comparison/Contrast

In a compare/contrast essay, you may choose this basic structure:

1. Describe one subject

2. Describe the other subject

3. Identify the similarities in the two subjects

4. Identify the differences in the two subjects

Argument

In an essay in which you are asked to argue a particular position, you may create an outline like this:

1. Statement of overall position

2. Series of paragraphs, each with a different specific argument for the overall position along with supporting evidence

3. One or more paragraphs that describe and dispute counter-arguments

Evaluation

An evaluation essay is often organized in this way:

1. Description of the topic and the criteria used to evaluate it (often in the introduction)

2. Series of paragraphs, each restating one of the criteria and describing how the topic meets that criterion based on evidence

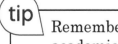

tip Remember, in addition to the body (main part), academic papers generally need to include an introduction and a conclusion.

Doing Research

Many writing assignments require students to explore and rport on what experts have said about a particular topic. Sometimes limited research is sufficient to gather some background information for a short assignment, while other times, extensive research is required – for example, for writing a research paper or thesis. For either, it is important to know how to do research effectively. Here are some tips for doing academic research:

Limit the scope of your topic. Based on the writing assignment, limit your research to a particular aspect of the subject you want to cover. The scope should not be too broad (covering more than the required areas) nor too narrow (not meeting the substantial requirement of a research scope).

Recognize the difference between primary and secondary research. Primary research involves reading through original documents such as newspaper articles, court documents, or personal letters. In the fields of math or science, it means conducting new scientific, medical, or engineering experiments. Secondary research, on the other hand, involves gathering information by reading others' research. Which type you do will be determined by the requirements of the writing assignment.

Find good sources of information. One of the best ways to find sources of information is the bibliography or list of sources used at the end of a journal article or book on your subject.

Librarians are great resources for research; they can tell you the best places to find information on your topic both in the library and online.

Determine the credibility and timeliness of each source. For academic research, peer-reviewed journals are considered reliable sources because each article must undergo a rigorous review process in which the accuracy of the information and the rigor of experimental process is verified. When looking at sources, consider these questions:

- Does my evidence come from sources that my readers (e.g., your peers and professors) and I trust?

- Do I have enough support for my claim, or am I making generalizations based on one or two examples?

- Are the statistics, information, and examples I am using recent? Are they still accurate and relevant?

Making Notes

As you research, note exactly where each piece of information comes from, including the author, title, date, and volume number or website URL. If you wait until later to record this information, you could make a mistake in your citations. With online sites, the article could even be taken down by the time you return.

tip

Wikipedia is rarely seen by professors as a worthy source for academic papers. You can look at this site to get very general information about a subject, but do not use it as a source for your paper.

Citing Sources

When you use information from journals, books, websites, and other sources for your papers and presentations, you need to cite those sources. Correct citation of sources is an essential part of academic writing and a critical step in avoiding plagiarism. Although there are numerous citation styles, some of the most common are:

> AMA: medicine, health and biological sciences
>
> APA: psychology, education and other social sciences
>
> Chicago: all subjects
>
> CSE: sciences
>
> MLA: literature, arts and humanities

Here is an example of an in-text citation in APA style:

The social ecological model, in that it addresses health from the individual, interpersonal, organizational, community and policy levels, has a greater impact than models that take a narrow, one-dimensional view of the influences on health behaviors (Patrick, 2013).

Each style has its set of very specific rules about the use of punctuation, capitalization, spacing, and fonts. These rules can be found online, such as at *The Chicago Manual of Style Online*, as well as in published materials like the *Publication Manual of the American Psychological Association*.

Reference Lists

In addition to citing sources within the text, you must include a full list of your sources at the end of each paper in the bibliography. Again, the format of the references depends on the citation style. Here are some examples of references in APA style:

Journal article:

> White, C. (2014). *Seeing things: Science, the fourth dimension, and modern enchantment.* The American Historical Review, 119(5), 1466-1491.

Book:

> Rogers, E.M. (2003). *Diffusion of innovations* (5th ed.). New York: Free Press.

Website material:

> Centers for Disease Control. (2013). Severe Acute Respiratory Syndrome (SARS). Retrieved from http://www.cdc.gov/SARS/

Reporting Source Information

Much of what you will write in academic papers, especially research papers, involves reporting information that other researchers and writers have published. Here are some words and phrases commonly used to report information obtained from outside sources:

When the source provides information: *note, observe, report*

> The authors **note** that "translating the results from statistical models into meaningful outcomes is not always straightforward."

> Swichtenberg **observes**, "Numerous polls show that Americans don't want to be told where they can and cannot travel."

> The CDC **reports** that the rate of premature births in that state has dropped significantly since 2008.

When the source explains: *discuss, explain*

> The article **discusses** important insights on the popularity of Twitter and its significance for journalism.

In the report, Traven **explains** that "affect" is a general term encompassing a broad range of feelings that individuals experience.

When the source expresses an opinion: *believe, declare, from X's point of view, in X's opinion*

Nash **believes** that the inability to pass immigration legislation was a policymaking failure.

The researchers **declare** that until more studies are conducted, no policy changes should be made.

From Wollenzein's point of view, the growing trend in vaccine refusal presents a serious health threat.

In Sherrer's opinion, print media in various countries should differ systematically in the kind of mediated deliberation they offer.

When the source presents an argument: *argue, assert, claim*

The authors a**rgue** that the role women have played in the founding of the country has been overlooked by textbook writers.

Unzicker **asserts** that organized crime depends on financial secrecy.

Manning **claims** that the virus can be spread through casual contact.

When the source provides evidence: *demonstrate, show*

Holmes **demonstrates** that when studied together, these topics reveal important relationships between architecture and suburbia.

Reyes **shows** that neither of the interventions made a significant impact on the participants' behavior.

Choosing the Right Words

To choose the right words, think about the characteristics of words, such as uncountable vs. countable nouns and formal vs. informal words. The following common words are uncountable nouns that are used in the singular, **not** in the plural.

Advice

*I am applying for an internship in Bangladesh this summer. Do you have any **advice** on how to write a cover letter?*

Evidence

*The recommendations are based on **evidence** from a number of studies on ways to encourage women to access antenatal health services.*

Feedback

*The evaluation surveys provided valuable **feedback** for improving the quality of the program.*

Funding

*We hope to receive **funding** for the project from USAID.*

Homework

*I have a lot of **homework** to do this weekend.* Note: "Homework assignments" can also be used (e.g., *That professor gives a lot of homework assignments.*).

Information

*Where can I find **information** on the art of Phillippe-Auguste Hennequin?*

Knowledge

*It is critical that **knowledge** gained from epidemiological studies be shared with those working in the field.*

Literature

*I have read much of the **literature** on that particular philosophy, but have not found any substantial criticism against it.*

Research

*Dr. Michaux has done **research** on the organizational patterns of research articles.*

Understanding

*The speaker has a profound **understanding** of issues related to mental health problems among returning veterans.*

tip A thesaurus contains lists of synonyms (words that have the same or similar meanings). A thesaurus was traditionally a print book, but it is now a common tool in word processing programs. You can also find thesauruses free online. A thesaurus is wonderful tool for effective writing for native and non-native English speakers alike. It helps writers increase variety in writing and choose the exact word to express intended meaning. For a non-native English speaker, using a thesaurus regularly can also help you increase your vocabulary — look up unfamiliar words in a dictionary.

Formality

Academic writing is more formal than other types of writing, so substitute formal words in your papers for the less formal ones you use in conversation. For example, in informal writing or speaking, we often use contractions (e.g., *can't, isn't, hasn't*); however, these are avoided in academic writing. In addition, refrain from using phrasal verbs (two- or three-word verbs) in formal writing; instead, choose one-word verbs. Here are some examples:

Phrasal Verb	One-Word Verb
Ask for	Request
Bring about	Produce, cause
Call off	Cancel
Cut down on	Reduce
Deal with	Manage
Find out	Ascertain, determine
Look into	Investigate
Look over	Examine
Put off	Postpone
Set up	Establish
Wipe out	Eliminate

Here are more words and phrases that have a similar meaning but different levels of formality. Use the informal version in speaking and the formal version in writing:

Informal	Formal
a lot of	a significant number of, many, much
besides	apart from
but	however, nevertheless
enough	sufficient
finish	complete
get	obtain
hard, tough	challenging, difficult
in addition to that	in addition

later on	later
so	therefore, thus
since	because
start	begin
think	believe
work	operate, function

Using Effective Writing Practices

There are a number of effective practices to help ensure high quality writing. Developing organized paragraphs, for example, is critical for good writing. A paragraph is a group of sentences related to a single controlling idea. Paragraphs help the reader see the organization of the essay and note its main points. Most paragraphs in an essay have an introduction and a body, and each part plays an important role:

Introduction: Includes the topic sentence and other sentences that give background information or provide a transition.

Body: Supports the topic or controlling idea using facts, examples, arguments, analysis, and other information.

Topic Sentences

A topic sentence helps organize a paragraph by telling what the rest of the paragraph is about. The topic sentence is usually the first or second sentence in a paragraph. The sentences that follow give more information about the topic by describing it, offering facts about it, or providing evidence for it. A topic sentence must be general enough to express the paragraph's overall subject, but specific enough that the paragraph's main subject and point are clear.

Note the topic sentence in this example:

Blogs have become a popular way to share information and express ideas and opinions. A blog is a regularly updated website written in an informal or conversational style. Blogs emerged in the late 1990s and have grown as the technology used to post information has become more user-friendly. A typical blog combines text, images, and links, and most blog sites allow readers to leave comments – a feature that distinguishes blogs from other websites. The rise in popularity of blogs has led to new terms in the English language, including "blog" as a noun (the site) and a verb (the action of updating a blog with new content) and "blogger" (a person who blogs.)

The first sentence is the topic sentence, and it introduces the topic of blogs. The sentences that follow provide further information about the topic.

Creating Flow

When a paper flows well, it has a clear and logical organization and reads smoothly. A clear structure and transitions help your paper flow. Problems with flow are common; you may find comments on your paper from your instructor that include words such as: "choppy," "jumpy," "lacking coherence." To improve flow, look at two elements of your writing: structure and transitions. Structure is the order in which the different parts of your discussion or argument are presented, and transitions are words and phrases that show relationships between the parts.

Structure

The organization of your paper depends on a number of factors, including purpose and length. Most academic and professional documents follow a specific structure; you can find out more about what the structure of your paper should look like from your instructor's instructions and from looking at examples of the type of text you are writing.

Transitions

Transitions signal relationships between ideas and provide the reader with directions for how to piece together your ideas into a logically coherent argument.

Transitions between Sections

Transitional paragraphs summarize the information just covered and specify the relevance of this information to the discussion in the following section.

> **tip**
>
> Many schools have writing centers where you can get help on all aspects of writing, including organizing your paper and making effective transitions to connect ideas.

Transitions between Paragraphs

Transitions can connect paragraphs through a word, phrase, or a sentence, and can come at the end of the first paragraph, at the beginning of the second paragraph, or both.

Transitions within Paragraphs

As with transitions between sections and paragraphs, transitions within paragraphs show relationships between ideas. Within paragraphs, transitions tend to be single words or short phrases.

Here are some connecting words and phrases along with examples of their use:

• **To add more information, use words like:** *also, furthermore, in addition* and *moreover.*

Improved school culture, stronger administrative support, and increased preparation have all been linked to improved retention of instructors. Mentoring has **also** been identified as having the potential to reduce faculty attrition.

The researchers in the study did not make a sufficient effort to control for bias, nor did they address the issue in their report. **Furthermore,** when members of the committee asked about potential bias, the researchers offered no response.

The survey showed that the women and men did not differ significantly in their values and hope for their lives and careers, and that a few of the businesswomen had left the workforce to take care of children. **In addition,** most of the women anticipated that their careers would rank equally with those of their partners.

Many educators see in hip hop the potential to promote learning of academic subjects. However, teachers should consider looking at this genre of music as a social and cultural practice. **Moreover,** music educators might provide opportunities for students to engage with hip hop musically and critically in the same way as they do other types of music.

• **To show consequences, you can use words like:** *as a result, consequently, for this reason, hence, therefore* and *thus.*

Many younger residents in the metropolitan area do not have landlines. **As a result,** researchers were not able to include those residents in the survey.

More and more, consumers are purchasing products that they see as environmentally friendly and as lowering future solar energy costs while reducing reliance on foreign oil supplies. **Consequently,** providing information about the environmental impact of different electricity products is critical for tapping into this growing market.

Size appears to be a reliable measure of bank-specific tail risk. **For this reason,** during the most recent U.S. recession, the hedged-size portfolio of commercial banks lost more than 100 cents on the dollar.

Many believe that depression is caused solely by a chemical imbalance and can only be treated with medication. **Hence,** many mental health professionals find it difficult to convince people to participate in behavioral therapy to address the problem.

This state adopted seatbelt laws earlier than many other states; **therefore,** the rate of car accident fatalities in the last several decades has been lower here than in other parts of the country.

Descriptions often fail to convey the richness and complexity of subsistence practices; **thus,** how to define "agriculturalists" and "hunter-gatherers" remains problematic.

- **To compare and contrast information, you can use words like:** *by contrast, nevertheless, rather, still* and *yet*

The two-week intervention program did not produce significant behavior change in any of the participants. **By contrast**, results from the six-week program showed that the majority of participants made meaningful and lasting changes in their behavior.

The building was designed by a famous French beaux-arts architect, **nevertheless;** the Palacio Ortiz Basualdo did not draw a great deal of attention at the time.

Beginning an exercise program that is very strenuous is not recommended; **rather,** doctors suggest starting slow and increasing the degree of difficulty over time.

At the end of the 1960s, the field of public administration included all of these groups with various lines of thought. **Still,** all groups did share one common creed: the belief in objective knowledge.

Michelangelo had no children, **yet** he became the father of many imitators who saw themselves as his successors.

- **To show similarity, you can use words like:** *likewise* and *similarly.*

Some of the teens stated that they did not want to participate in the study; **likewise,** many of those who participated in the beginning dropped out after a short time.

Small nonprofit organizations are struggling to continue their work despite a decrease in donations; **similarly,** large NGOs have had to cut costs due to decreased funding for ongoing projects.

- **To restate information in your own words, you can use words like:** *in other words* and *that is to say.*

Behavior change is difficult without a sense of self-efficacy; **in other words**, an individual must feel capable of making the desired change.

Providing student loans has a net positive effect on society; **that is to say,** society benefits from the socioeconomic mobility and the skilled work force that result from greater access to higher education.

• **To emphasize information, you can use words like:** *above all, chiefly, and especially*

The reviewers made many recommendations for improving the advertisements; **above all**, they said, the benefits of the product must be more strongly emphasized.

The physician offered many reasons that the medication should not be recommended for infants; **chiefly,** that its effects have not been studied in children under 5.

The training was very important for the research assistants, **especially** those who had limited experience in the field.

• **To show an exception, you can use words like:** *except* and *excluding.*

All of the strategies aimed to improve customer service except the last one, which addressed general management training modules only.

Excluding those who arrived late, all of the conference participants indicated that their level of knowledge had increased.

• **To provide examples, you can use words like:** *for example, including,* and *such as.*

Many museums have become successful through strategic branding. The Tate Modern, **for example,** is the most innovative and professionally branded museum in the world.

Psychopaths have been subjects of a great deal of research for a number of reasons, **including** that they are individuals that fail to understand the nature of moral considerations.

Several theories, **such as** social learning theory and the theory of planned behavior, could have been used as a framework for this study.

> **tip**
> Do not use *etc.* in academic writing. Using phrases like *such as, including* and *for example* indicates that there are other items or examples that are not named.

• **To summarize information, you can use words like:** *in conclusion* and *in summary*

In conclusion, the new regulations will not prevent the pharmaceutical companies from marketing drugs on television because...

In summary, "harshness" can be defined in a number of ways, including treatment that hurts offenders by depriving them of liberty or infringes on rights which they either have, or would have in circumstances in which they had committed no crime.

Grammatical Note

When connecting two clauses within a sentence using connecting words like *however, moreover* and *nevertheless*, the connecting word is preceded by a semicolon and followed by a comma.

Examples:

Marketing strategies have traditionally been used to sell commercial products; **nevertheless,** *these same strategies can be used to effectively promote positive health behavior change.*

Working with community partners can be time-consuming; **however,** *the quality of a community needs assessment depends on ensuring that community members participate in the process.*

Ensuring Parallelism and Consistency

When revising your paper, make sure elements of your writing are **parallel** and **consistent**. Parallelism in writing means using the same pattern of words each time. When you have a list, for instance, make sure each item on the list is the same type and form of word. Here are a couple of examples:

*Topics include **standard costing systems, cost volume-profit analysis,** and **short-term decision making**.* (The three items listed here are all nouns with modifiers.)

*The strategies employed in the youth health campaign included **forming** theater groups, **organizing** sports teams, **utilizing** volunteer peer counselors, and **recruiting** guest speakers for workshops and conferences.* (The four actions here are all verbs in the gerund form.)

Consistency in writing means ensuring that certain elements are uniform throughout a document, including tone, spelling, capitalization, formatting, and point of view.

Tone: The tone of the paper (e.g., formal, informal) should be the same throughout the paper.

Spelling: When there is a term that can be spelled more than one way, choose one way and be consistent. For example, you can write *health care,*healthcare,* or *health-care,* but whichever way you choose, spell it the same way throughout your paper.

*health care is the most common spelling.

Choose one dictionary, such as the Merriam-Webster dictionary online, to use as a reference for all your papers to ensure consistency.

Capitalization: When writing lists, be consistent with capitalization. If each item on your list is a complete sentence, begin with a capital letter and end with a period. If each item continues a sentence (as shown below), then begin each item with a lower-case letter. Use end punctuation only if you are finishing complete sentences.

Example:

The sales team will recruit customers through:

- phone calls
- emails
- brochures
  (None of the first words is capitalized.)

Formatting: Use the same formatting throughout a paper, including fonts, indentions, and spacing.

Point of View: If you use pronouns such as *I* or *we* in the paper (e.g., *In our research, we found that...*) use that same point of view throughout the paper.

Editing Your Paper

When you turn in a paper, your professor will expect that it is well organized and free of errors. So, while it takes time, revising is a critical part of writing and should be done before submission of any paper. To thoroughly edit your paper, begin with global (overall) revisions, then make local (specific) revisions. To make global revisions, ask yourself these questions:

Focus: Did I make and develop a central point? Did I develop my ideas thoroughly? Did I stay on track throughout the paper?

Organization: Does the development of my points follow a logical pattern? Do the transitions move readers sensibly from point to point? Would the paper work better if I moved some paragraphs around?

Audience: Did I spend too much time discussing material that most of my readers already know? Did I answer important questions that readers might have about my topic? Did I define all the concepts and terms my readers need to know?

Purpose: Did I make my intention clear? Did I develop all my intended points? Would a reader be able to summarize my paper easily?

Proportion: Are the parts of the paper in balance? Could my readers tell what points are most important by the amount of attention I've given to them?

Format: Have I used the right overall format (margins, font, title, headings)? Have I used the correct format for all citations? Are tables, charts, and images relevant, accurate, and legible?

Transitions: Have I used transitions to connect ideas between sentences, paragraphs, and sections to ensure that my paper flows?

Introduction and Conclusion: Is my introduction interesting and accurate? Does my conclusion provide a strong ending that pulls the whole paper together?

Local Revisions

The second stage of revising is identifying and correcting errors. Here are some common errors to look for:

Spelling Errors: Typical spelling errors include confusing homonyms like *it's* and *its* and *there, their,* and *they're.*

Capitalization Errors: Mistakes in capitalization often include failure to capitalize the first letter of important words in titles and headings.

Fragments: Typical fragments include introductory phrases like *When the novel was completed* that are not followed by a clause.

Run-on Sentences: A run-on sentence occurs when two or more complete sentences are connected improperly. This often results in long sentences that should be broken up into two or more sentences.

For example:

Other Hispanic populations have immigrated to the U.S. over the years, more than 12 million people in California speak Spanish as a first language.

An example of a correct version is: *Other Hispanic populations have immigrated to the U.S. over the years, and now more than 12 million people in California speak Spanish as a first language.*

Comma Splices: Comma splices occur when two sentences are joined by a comma (e.g., *The research assistants were trained to conduct the surveys, they practiced with each other.* An example of a correct version is: *The research assistants were trained to conduct the surveys, and they practiced with each other.*)

Incorrect Placement of Apostrophes: A common mistake is to put the apostrophe in the wrong place (e.g., *All of the student's desks were covered with papers.* The correct version is: *students'*)

Inaccurate Punctuation with Quotations: Put commas and periods inside quotation marks (e.g., *Dr. Stevens said, "It's time to go"*. The correct version is: *"to go."*)

Grammar mistakes made by non-native English speakers often include errors in the use of articles (*a, an, the*) and verb tenses. Information about these and all types of grammar issues can be found on numerous sites online.

Unit 4

Developing Your Career

RESUME

Career Objective:

Management Consultant with 20 years of experienc
objective advice, expertise and specialist skills with t
maximizing growth and improving business performa

Professional Experience:

- Over 20 years of in-depth experience in the interior
- Improved the accuracy of budget forecasts.
- Established good working relationsh
- Developed

Part 1: Getting Started

Because the process can be long, it is important to begin looking for career development opportunities as soon as possible. In addition to networking, you will need time for researching organizations and identifying available positions. This section will help you understand the steps involved in starting your career and the resources available to you along the way. Here you will find information and tips on:

- Utilizing Resources
- Networking
- Gaining Experience
- Meeting the Challenges

Utilizing Resources

Typically, student enroll in institutes of higher learning as a step toward successful careers. However, knowing how to move from school into the world of professional work can be daunting, especially for international students who want to work in the U.S. but may be unfamiliar with the process. Fortunately, most schools offer resources to support students' career development efforts. Probably the best resource is your school's office of career services, which is dedicated to helping students reach their career goals. In addition to one-one-one career counseling, career services often include:

- Networking events
- Mock (practice) interview sessions
- Résumé writing workshops
- Informational sessions on employment/immigration issues
- Career fairs
- Online databases of job opportunities

Other resources to take advantage of include:

Job Search Websites: Job search sites on the Internet list thousands of jobs every day.

Alumni: Alumni are some of the most valuable networking resource for current students. Because they are professionals currently working in the field, alumni often know of the kinds of opportunities that students are looking for. Some of the best ways to connect with alumni are through career services events and alumni databases, as well as social networking websites.

Faculty: Like alumni, professors are great resources for students looking to gain experience in the field. Many are engaged in research and projects inside and outside the school and can connect students with opportunities. However, many international students feel anxious about approaching professors and are not sure how to go about it. The best way to start is to email the professor and ask for an appointment. Here is an example:

Dear Dr. Styles,

My name is Adita Subramanium, and I am a student in your mechatronics class. I have enjoyed your lectures on intelligent control, and I would like to talk with you the possibility of working on your high efficiency robots project this summer. Would you be available for an appointment sometime in the next couple of weeks? I am in class every morning during the week, but I am free every afternoon.

Thank you so much,
Adita Subramanium

Networking

You will hear a lot about *networking* while you are in the U.S. Networking is about building relationships and is a key strategy for career development. When it comes to the world of work, there is some truth to the saying, "It's not *what* you know, but *who* you know." For that reason, networking – developing a set of contacts with whom you build relationships, share information, and provide support – is a critical part of career development. Networking can occur in both informal and formal ways, and a strong network comprises both professional and social connections. Informal social networks include friends and acquaintances, current and former coworkers, and people you meet at social events and activities. Formal networking involves joining groups, such as professional and alumni associations.

The idea of networking may be new to you and may even make you feel uncomfortable. In formal networking situations, you may feel nervous and like you don't know what to say. While we are all accustomed to being friendly and engaged with people we know, we see networking as a something like a job interview, so it's easy to think that we need to act differently. The good news is that you do not have to act in an unnatural or insincere way when networking. The best way to approach networking is simply to be friendly and curious.

Being Friendly

Remember that it is not up to others to seek you out; it is your job to be open and reach out to others to get things started. If you are at an event, offer a sincere compliment ("I've heard good things about your organization's work") or a friendly remark ("The food here is really great"). Be yourself, and focus on relaxing and being sociable. You may have to push yourself to be more outgoing than usual, but when you show others you are a warm and friendly person, they will be more open and relaxed with you as well.

Being Curious

Because you are trying to develop relationships with new people, focus on getting to know them. Instead of approaching networking with the sole objective of getting a job, simply try to find out more about other people. Networking is often more about listening to what people say than saying the right things; take the time to get to know people and connect with them. People like to talk about themselves, and when you show that you are interested in learning about their ideas, interests, and needs, they will be more interested in yours as well.

Following Up

One or two days after meeting someone with whom you would like to communicate further, follow up with a brief email. In the email, first remind the person who you are and where/when you met. You may want to bring up a topic that you discussed in your first encounter. You can use phrases such as: *I enjoyed...* or *I appreciated...* For example:

- *I enjoyed hearing about your research on semiconductor process modeling.*
- *I appreciated what you said about the challenges of entering a new market.*

Then, you can follow up on your conversation by asking for the opportunity to meet again, for information about how to contact someone you spoke about, or news about job opportunities. Here is an example of a follow-up email:

Dear Ms. Johnson,

My name is Xin Sun, and I am a second-year law student at X University. I am from China and met you last Friday evening at the Alumni Association dinner. I really enjoyed hearing about your organization's work on international trade in endangered species.

As I mentioned in our conversation, I hope to do some work after graduation on my country's policies regarding the illegal trade of ivory. I see from your website that your agency funds a project that is working on this issue in Shanghai. I was wondering if you know whom I might contact to find out more about that project.

Thank you so much,
Xin Sun

As you follow up with people you meet, be conscientious. In particular, be sensitive to other people's time constraints and obligations. Keep your communications brief and to the point. Instead of sending a long, five-paragraph explanation of why you are contacting them, use that first email to focus on a small point or question. You can then send further details if they reply.

Gaining Experience

One of the factors employers consider when considering job applicants is work experience. Unfortunately, because young people in many countries are less likely to work while in school, international students often lack significant work experience. There are ways, however, to gain practical experience while studying in the U.S. Doing volunteer work and/or unpaid internships offer the opportunity to both network and obtain key skills that will be of interest to potential employers. In addition, working as a volunteer in a professional setting provides evidence to others of your ability to:

- Take on a leadership role
- Balance tasks and responsibilities
- Deliver on commitments
- Set priorities
- Work with a team
- Communicate effectively with a variety of people in a variety of contexts

CPT and OPT

One way international students can gain work experience is to get training during school or after graduation through Curricular Practical Training (CPT) or Optional Practical Training (OPT).

Curricular Practical Training (CPT)

Following the completion of one full academic year as a full-time student, students with F-1 visas may apply for paid practical experience in their field of study. This practical training is considered part of the student's academic curriculum and is known as Curricular Practical Training (CPT).

Optional Practical Training (OPT)

Optional Practical Training (OPT) is available both during the program of study and after graduation. It is limited to a part-time position while classes are in session, but may be authorized for a full-time position during the summer vacation or during other periods when classes are not in session.

To learn all the details about OPT and CPT programs, contact your school's Office of Career Services or Office of International Student and Scholar Services.

Meeting the Challenges

In order to set realistic expectations, international students need to understand the challenges to finding a job in the U.S. Many international students come to the U.S. to earn a degree and then return to their country to take up professional positions at home. Others hope to remain after graduation and find work in the U.S. However, those seeking work in the U.S. often find it takes more effort than expected. Three of the main reasons are:

> 1. Many positions funded by federal, state, and local governments are only open to applicants with a certain immigration status, usually permanent U.S. residents and citizens.

> 2. Some international students lack a sufficient degree of oral and writing proficiency in English to compete for jobs with native speakers of English.

> 3. International students often enter graduate programs immediately after completing undergraduate school and therefore have a limited amount of work experience.

In addition, companies who hire an international student/graduate often have to sponsor the employee, a process that requires a substantial investment of time and money. Companies are particularly reluctant to sponsor an employee if they believe he or she may not stay with the company for an extended period of time.

Despite the challenges, international students can find work in the U.S. Here are some tips:

• Take advantage of career services

Career services offices are there to help students reach their career goals. Career services staff are experts at all aspects of the job search — from writing effective résumés to finding career opportunities to successfully handling job interviews. Career services often include one-one-one career counseling, networking events, and workshops on issues related to immigration and employment.

• Engage in activities outside the classroom

While academic achievement is certainly important, employers in the U.S. are also interested in what students have done outside the classroom. Participating in clubs, student government, sports, or other activities shows that you can do more than just academic work. Volunteer work, in particular, shows your willingness to invest time in working for the benefit of others, and is a chance to gain critical work experience.

• Be persistent and don't get discouraged!

Looking for a job can be a long, tedious, and time-consuming process for *everyone*. That is why you must be persistent and to continue to network and look for opportunities to grow your own skills and experience. It is easy to become discouraged, but if you continue to make the effort, the chances are better that your hard work will pay off!

Part 2: Selling Yourself

As you identify career opportunities, such as jobs and internships, you will need to be able to show decision makers why you are the best candidate for the position. Effectively communicating your particular knowledge, experience, skills, and talents – both in person and in writing – is critical. This section will help you "sell yourself" so that you have the best chance of making a positive impression on potential employers and others. Here you will find information and tips on:

- Creating a Résumé
- Writing Cover Letters
- Communicating by Email
- Developing an Elevator Speech
- Interviewing

Creating a Résumé

A résumé is a summary of your education, experience, and skills, and is used to introduce yourself to prospective employers. A résumé is similar to a curriculum vitae (CV), but is a shorter document that includes only the more pertinent information. To make a good impression, it is important that your résumé is well written. While different versions can be tailored to the position for which you are applying, your résumé should include contact information, education, and experience. Education includes the degrees you have earned, the year you earned each degree, and the name and location of each school. Experience includes both paid (professional) and unpaid work (e.g., volunteer work and internships). For each position you have held, you will need to indicate:

- Your job title
- The organization's name
- The dates you worked for the organization
- A description of your roles and responsibilities

List all experience chronologically, starting with the most recent. All related work experience counts and should be included on your résumé, no matter whether the experience was gained in the U.S. or in your country. Use the simple past tense on your résumé for describing your previous experience and the simple present tense to describe your current work, if applicable.

In addition to these sections, there are optional sections you may include, including:

- Professional Memberships
- Research/Publications
- Presentations
- Certifications
- Honors and Awards
- Extracurricular Activities
- International Experience
- Special Skills

Do not include photos or personal information such as age, marital status, ethnicity, or religious affiliation on your résumé.

Here are some guidelines for **résumé** formatting:

Font Size: 10 to 12pt.

Font Type: Times New Roman, Calibri, or Arial

Margins: Between 0.5" and 1.0"

Paper: For paper versions, use quality bond paper that is 8.5 x11", white or off-white.

When you email a **résumé** to an employer, it's important to follow their guidelines. Some organizations will indicate how they want the **résumé** sent – either in the body of the email or as an attachment. When emailing your cover letter and résumé, title the documents with your last name and the organization and position name.

Example:

Wang_Microsoft_Programmer_Cover

Wang_Microsoft_Programmer_Résumé

The body of the email should include a brief note indicating why you're writing and that your cover letter and résumé are attached. Here is an example:

Dear Dr. Robinson,

I am applying for the position of Programmer in Microsoft's Cloud Services Division. Please find attached my résumé and cover letter.

Sincerely,
Yu Wang

References

You may or may not be asked for a list of references by a potential employer, but it is a good idea to have one ready, just in case. The reference list should comprise the names and contact information for three or four references and be printed on a separate page that has the same header as your résumé. You can ask for references from:

- Previous employers or supervisors
- Professors or university staff who know you
- Friends and colleagues, but **not** family (however, employers or university professionals would be better choices than friends)

Name	
Street Number and Name • City, State Zip Code	
(Area Code) Phone Number • Email Address	
EDUCATION	Name of School, City, State
	Month Year
	Degree
EXPERIENCE	Name of Organization, City, State
	Month Year — Month Year
	Title, Activity
PROFESSIONAL MEMBERSHIPS	Name of Organization
PUBLICATIONS	Publication information
PRESENTATIONS	Name of Presentation, Name of Event,
	Month Year
HONORS AND AWARDS	Name of Honor/Award, Name of Awarding
	Organization, Month Year
CERTIFICATIONS	Type of Certification, Name of Certifying
	Organization, Month Year
RESEARCH EXPERIENCE	Type of Research, Name of Organization,
	Month Year (Research Advisor: Name)
TECHNICAL KNOWLEDGE	Name of Software
VOLUNTEER ACTIVITIES	Title, Organization,
	Month Year - Month
	Year Description of activity
EXTRACURRICULAR ACTIVITIES	Title, Organization,
	Month Year - Month Year
	Description of activity

Education

- Include the country where you went to school if not in the U.S.
- If you haven't graduated yet, list the graduation date as "Expected." For example, "Expected May 2017."
- Include summer courses at the university level, including English language study.
- Do not include high school, unless you are a first-year university student and have very little to put on your resume to fill the page.

Experience

Describe all paid and unpaid experience directly related to your field. You don't need to mention jobs that are not related to what you are applying for (unless that is the only experience you have).

If there is no information to include in one of the sections above, omit that section.

Using Action Words

On your résumé and other written documents for potential employers, use action words to describe your experience. Here are some examples (in the simple past tense; look up unfamiliar words in your dictionary or online):

Achievement

Achieved	Earned
Acquired	Obtained
Attained	Reached
Completed	

Budgeting

Balanced	Estimated
Budgeted	Generated
Calculated	Reconciled
Computed	Tabulated

Consultation/Support

Advised	Encouraged
Assisted	Guided
Briefed	Participated in
Consulted	Provided
Counseled	Referred
Enabled	Supported

Communications

Authored	Prepared
Communicated	Produced
Composed	Promoted
Documented	Published
Developed	Synthesized
Drafted	Summarized
Edited	Wrote
Informed	

Development/Design

Built	Formulated
Constructed	Founded
Created	Initiated
Designed	Introduced
Developed	Launched
Devised	Planned
Established	Proposed

Education/Training

Facilitated	Presented
Illustrated	Taught
Instructed	Tutored
Lectured	Trained

Improvement

Adapted	Modified
Consolidated	Reduced
Decreased	Reorganized
Eliminated	Restructured
Enhanced	Revised
Expanded	Revitalized
Expedited	Simplified
Extended	Strengthened
Grew	Streamlined
Improved	Systematized
Increased	Updated
Integrated	Upgraded

Evaluation

Assessed	Evaluated
Critiqued	Tested

Leadership

Assigned	Implemented
Chaired	Led
Controlled	Piloted
Directed	Recruited
Employed	Supervised
Enforced	Oversaw
Headed	

Management/Administration

Coordinated	Scheduled
Handled	Catalogued
Maintained	Collected
Monitored	Compiled
Operated	Conducted
Organized	Examined
Recorded	Explored
Regulated	Investigated
Reported	Researched
Retrieved	Studied

Writing Cover Letters

A cover letter accompanies a résumé, highlighting your qualifications and demonstrating your strong interest in the position. The primary purpose of the cover letter is to convince the reader to look at your résumé. The letter should be tailored specifically for the position you are applying for; call attention to your relevant skills and experience; and reflect a positive attitude.

Before writing a cover letter, do two things:

Research the organization (via its website, annual reports, personal contacts)

In your letter, you want to demonstrate that you understand the needs of the organization and can contribute to its particular mission or goals.

Look carefully at the job description Identify the main qualifications the employer is seeking and the main duties of the position, and then examine your résumé to determine where you have developed these skills. In your letter, highlight those areas in which you have the relevant strengths. These days, many organizations can cover letters with a computer program that looks for key words – the important ones mentioned in the position announcement. Do your best to include those words in your cover letter too.

Parts of a Cover Letter

A cover letter usually contains three to four paragraphs with the following information:

Introduction (1 Paragraph)

Address the reader directly, using his or her title and last name, such as "Dear Dr. Robinson" or "Dear Ms. Matar" followed by a comma. If you cannot find the contact name in the job posting, on the website or by contacting the organization, then use

"Dear Sir/Madam."

The first section of your cover letter tells the reader who you are and why you are writing. Identify which position you are applying for, as there may be several available within an organization. It's also a good idea to state where you learned about the position, such as a website or listserv. If you were referred by someone you know within the organization, mention this in the first sentence (e.g., "I was referred to you by Ralph Strate regarding the Project Coordinator position.")

> **tip** Have a native English speaker proofread each résumé and cover letter before you send it to a prospective employer.

Professional Background (2-3 Paragraphs)

The majority of your letter should highlight your skills and experience that are directly related to the position. Don't summarize your entire work history; that information is on your resume. Instead, note your key qualifications for the position. Demonstrate how you acquired your relevant competencies through specific examples.

Closing (1 Paragraph)

In the final paragraph, you should sound enthusiastic about the position, telling your potential employer why you are eager to work for them. Include your contact information and thank the reader.

tip When sending more than one letter, make sure that the names and position titles of each recipient are accurate.

Name
Address
Phone Number
Email Address

Date

Name of Employer
Position
Organization
Address

Dear Title Last Name,

I am writing to apply for the position of (Position) within the (Department) of (Organization) that I learned about from (source). I have experience in (X), and I am currently earning a (Degree) at (School). Given my experience and training, I believe I am a competitive candidate for this position.

2-3 paragraphs describing your background and qualifications for the position

I hope to have the opportunity to work with (Organization) to help you achieve your (mission/goal) of (description of mission/goal), and I would welcome the opportunity to discuss the position with you further. I have attached my résumé for your review, and I can be reached at (phone number) or (email address). I look forward to speaking with you, and thank you for your consideration.

Sincerely,

Name

Communicating by Email

Looking for practicums, internships, fellowships, and employment opportunities often involves corresponding in a formal way via email. All messages should be polite, brief, and free of errors in spelling, punctuation, and grammar. Here are some phrases you can use for formal email communication:

Salutations

Dear Dr. Smith,

Dear Mr. Chau,

Dear Ms. Perera,

Beginning

My name is _____ and I am a student at _____ in the department of _____.

Request for Information

I am writing in reference to the position of (_____) in the department of _____, posted on your organization's website.

Offer to Send Information

Should you need any further information, please do not hesitate to contact me.

Conclusion

Thank you very much for your consideration.

Closing

Sincerely,

Developing an Elevator Speech

An elevator speech is a short speech that effectively describes a person, business, or idea. It is called an elevator speech (or an elevator pitch) because you could give the speech to someone in the time it takes to ride together in an elevator. The idea of an elevator speech is to quickly make the listener aware of your specific, unique, and impressive qualities. It is a way to let those you meet know where you've been and where you're hoping to go in the future. You can use your elevator speech in a number of situations, such as at:

Career fairs and networking events – to introduce yourself to potential employers

Interviews – in response to: *Tell me about yourself.*

Professional and social meetings – when you are asked to introduce yourself

The structure of an elevator speech for a job-hunter generally follows this pattern:

- Introduce yourself.
- Describe one or two specific strengths, skills, and/or professional experiences.
- State your goals and/or plans for the future.

tip Make sure to practice many times so you are comfortable delivering your elevator speech.

Here are a couple of examples of elevator speeches:

> My name is Harisha Gupta. I'm an entomologist with over five years of experience working in programs in the state of Uttar Pradesh to prevent vector-borne diseases, including malaria and dengue fever. I'm currently earning a Master's in Public Health at the University of X so that I may gain further skills in public health, particularly in surveillance. Once I graduate, I plan to continue my contributions to the alleviation of the burden of vector-borne diseases in India through the strengthening of surveillance systems.

> Hi, I'm Alex Akulov. I'm graduating in May with a Bachelor's Degree in Computer Science from X University, and would like to use the skills I have developed in a full-time software design position after I graduate. I've read about the advanced technologies your company used to develop the X, which I used on a software design project I worked on with Dr. X. The project won the X award last year. I noted that you'll be interviewing on campus next month, and I've submitted my resume in the hope that I can obtain an interview for your Database Systems Analyst position. I'm very interested to know more about your needs for this position.

Interviewing

Before offering an applicant a position, most employers require an interview. To do well in the interview, it is essential to be prepared. Learn as much as you can about the company – and interviewer if possible – in advance, and practice answers to job potential interview questions as well. Be prepared to look your best: get a haircut if necessary, make sure your clothing (business attire) is clean and pressed, and get a good night's sleep. Here are a few other things you can do to make a good impression:

The Morning of the Interview

- Take a shower and wash your hair.
- Refrain from wearing perfume/cologne.
- Use deodorant/antiperspirant.
- Make sure your nails are clean and trimmed.
- Brush your teeth and make sure your breath is fresh.

Upon Arriving at the Interview

- Be on time.
- Turn off your cell phone.
- Dispose of chewing gum.

During the Interview

- Sit up straight.
- Maintain eye contact.
- Stay positive and friendly.

> **tip** In video interviews, present yourself as you would in an in-person interview (professional dress, etc.) and make sure there is visible behind you or around you that would be inappropriate for an interview. For telephone or Skype interviews, find a quiet place where you will not be disturbed while you are talking.

At the End of the Interview

- Shake hands firmly and thank the interviewer.
- Ask about next steps.
- Request the interviewer's business card.

After the Interview

- Send the interviewer a thank-you note by email.

Sample Thank You Note

Dear Mr. Strother,

Thank you very much for meeting with me yesterday. I enjoyed learning more about your organization's obesity programs and having the opportunity to share further details of my training in physical education at X University. I am confident that the knowledge and skills I have acquired in the development and evaluation of physical education and nutrition programs match well with the position of health educator.

If there is any more information I can provide, please do not hesitate to let me know.

Sincerely,
Jing Lin

Interview Questions

One of the most common ways interviewers begin is by asking you to "Tell me about yourself." Generally, the interviewer wants to get to know you and determine if you are a good a fit for the organization. In response, give a general overview of yourself – where you are from, a brief summary of your background, and what you are doing now. You can also use this as an opportunity to mention work and school experiences you want the interviewer to know about.

Here are some other common types of interview questions, as well as tips for answering them effectively:

Tell me what makes you qualified for this job. The interviewer will probably talk about the specific role, responsibilities and tasks of the job, and will want to hear more about how prepared you are to take the position. Show that you understand what is involved in the position and how the job for calls for the skills and experience you possess.

What are your strengths and weaknesses? Questions about your strengths are used to help determine if you have some of the key skills for the job, while the weaknesses question is to assess your awareness of your shortcomings.

In terms of strengths, plan to talk about your top two or three skills that directly relate to the specific position you are applying for. In terms of weaknesses, it is important not to talk about issues that may hinder your job performance. Think about something that you recognize could get in the way of being productive, and tell the interviewer about ways you have learned to overcome or manage the issue successfully.

Why are you applying for this position? The interviewer wants to know how much you know about the job, what motivates you, and how much you want the specific job that is available.

Find out all you can about the job beforehand. Make a note of the aspects of the job that particularly match your skills and interests, and talk about those. You want to show that you understand what the position involves and that you are enthusiastic about getting started.

Where do you see yourself five years from now? When interviewers ask this question, they want to get a better understanding of your level of focus and commitment, to ensure that this position fits well with your overall goals.

Focus initially on what you would do in the current position and then relate those activities and experiences to your long-term career goals.

Here are a few more questions that are often asked in job interviews:

- *How do other people describe you?*
- *How do you prefer to be supervised?*
- *What changes can you envision making to (the organization/program)?*

Situational Interview Questions

In addition to finding out about your background, it is common for interviewers to ask situation questions that are designed to determine how you behave under challenging circumstances. Situational questions often start with *Tell me about a time when you...*The interviewer will ask you to reflect upon your previous work and school experiences and explain how you handled a particular situation. These questions usually ask about how you handled a difficult teammate or coworker, dealt with disappointment or failure, demonstrated leadership, or acted in a creative way to solve a challenging problem. The idea is to get a sense of the way you think, your values, and your ability to navigate difficult situations. Some examples of situational interview questions are:

Tell me about a time when you...

- *made a mistake at work/in school. How did you handle it?*

- *had a teammate who did not do his/her share of the work. How did you deal with it?*

- *started down one path but had to change course. How did you handle it?*

- *had a disagreement with your supervisor. How did you deal with it?*

- *received negative feedback from a supervisor. What did you do with the information?*

- *did not have all of the resources you needed to complete a project. How did you handle it?*

> **tip**
>
> In the U.S., there are some questions that interviewers are not allowed to ask. These questions are generally related to personal issues, such as: *How old are you? Are you married? How many kids do you have? What religion do you practice? Do you have any disabilities?* Feel free to refrain from answering these types of questions, and be wary of any employer who would ask for this type of information, as the practice is prohibited by law.

Preparing for Situational Interview Questions

Before the interview, think about challenging situations at work/school in which you handled problems and prepare to talk in detail about a few experiences. Focus on what specific actions you took to manage the problem and produce a successful outcome. You can do what is called a "STAR" analysis:

S = Name a SITUATION you faced or

T= a TASK you had to complete.

A= Describe what ACTION you took and

R= the RESULTS of your actions.

In the interview, you can use this structure answering the questions.

Unit 5:

Furthering Your Education

Many international students decide to go on to pursue another degree before entering the workforce full time. Many of the same steps in applying for acceptance into an academic program are similar to those for applying for a job, including creating a résumé and filling out applications. There are other steps as well, such as requesting recommendation letters and writing a statement of purpose. This section looks at applying for a master's or doctoral level degree program. Here you will find information and tips on:

- Writing a Statement of Purpose
- Requesting Recommendation Letters
- Interviewing

Writing a Statement of Purpose

When applying for academic and other types of programs, you will probably be asked to submit a statement of purpose (or personal essay) that describes yourself and your reasons for applying. A statement of purpose should present a clear, positive picture of who you are and of how acceptance to the program will help you achieve your goals. The objective is to persuade an admissions committee that you are an applicant they should choose. You want to show that you have the experience, knowledge, skills, and motivation to succeed in your chosen field. Here are the steps in the process of writing a statement of purpose:

Look at Examples: Read several examples (e.g., from the Internet) and pay attention to the qualities of a good essay. Use the good ones as models, not for content but for structure and flow.

Develop an Outline: Select the main topics you want to cover and list supporting material under each topic. Only include information about your past that helps to explain how you came to focus on your current interests and objectives. Below are some examples of relevant information:

- **Personal Background** (difficulties overcome; extra-curricular achievements; unusual life situations that may have influenced your aspirations)

- **Educational Background** (relevant classes taken; specific projects undertaken; specific skills acquired)

- **Professional Goals** (why you want to be an X; what specific area of the field you want to get into; what you plan to do with your degree)

- **Program Choice** (why you want to attend X university/program in particular; why you are a good candidate for this particular program)

- **Research Experience** (include title of project, collaborators, your responsibilities, outcomes)

- **Work Experience** (demonstrates knowledge of the

field and/or indicates interest in the work of those in the program/department to which you are applying)

- **Achievements** (prizes, awards, nominations, fellowships)

Write a Rough Draft: Transform your outline into a first draft. Consider the following when writing:

- **Beginning:** Start your essay with something that will grab the readers' attention and engage them, such as an anecdote (very brief story) or a question you want to answer.
- **Middle:** The entire document should flow together in a logical order (e.g., chronological; academic work first then applied work). Use transitions between paragraphs that contribute to the flow and organization of your writing (e.g., *soon afterwards, as a result of, building on that experience*).
- **End:** End your essay with a conclusion that restates the main idea in the first paragraph.

Edit Carefully: Put your draft away for a day or two, then reread it and edit it as many times as possible. Send your statement to a native English speaker to give you feedback and proofreading.

> **tip**
>
> The personal statement is an opportunity to highlight your positive attributes; it is *not* a place to make any negative statements about poor grades or difficulty with English, for example. Of course you must be truthful, but the personal statement is not a place to downplay your achievements to seem modest. Be proud of all that you have accomplished!

Requesting Recommendation Letters

You will likely be required to provide recommendation letters from faculty as part of your application. Although asking a professor for a letter of recommendation may cause anxiety, remember that this is a regular part of a professor's job. When deciding which faculty member to approach, think about a professor from whom you have taken more than one class; in whose classes you have done well; and/or who can comment upon your intellectual abilities and skills. Once you have chosen the professor(s) to ask, here are some tips:

Ask Early

Faculty members are very busy, and, although they may be happy to write you a letter, you need to give them as much time as possible. You can make the request in person or via email. Here is a sample email:

Dear Dr. Goss,

Good afternoon. I wanted to let you know that I have decided to apply for the Ph.D. in Biological Chemistry program at X University for the fall. I am very excited about the possibility of working with the faculty there on projects examining nano materials synthesis and reactions.

I would like to know if you would be comfortable writing me a letter of recommendation. If so, I can send you all the relevant materials and information. The application is due March 1.

Thank you, and I look forward to your reply.

Naser Al Moklif

Provide the Relevant Information

If your professor agrees to write the recommendation, he/she will need to know a lot about you, the program you are applying to, and why you are interested in that particular program. Therefore, you should provide him/her with:

- Your résumé
- Your statement of purpose
- Information about the program

You may also want to provide copies of papers or projects you have worked on that demonstrate your relevant skills.

In addition, you need to provide the key submission information, including:

- Submission format (e.g., upload a .pdf; send an email with letter attached; fill out an online form)
- The title, name and address of the person to whom the letter is to be addressed
- The submission deadline

Follow Up

If you find, about one week before the due date, that the professor has not submitted the letter, you can send a friendly reminder. Also, don't forget to thank the professor for the recommendation. A brief email is usually sufficient, but a personal thank-you note is even better. Finally, let your professor know the outcome of your application.

Interviewing

Many academic programs will ask you to do an interview. It is important to think about potential questions and carefully prepare your answers. It is a good idea to think about the same topics that you wrote about in your personal statement, including what has led you to this point in your academic career and what contribution you hope to make to the field. You will also want to find out as much as you can about the program to which you are applying. Specifically, it is a good idea to learn about:

- The details of the program
- Which faculty are doing work in your area of interest
- Projects the professors are working on
- What other students in the program are doing

Many of the questions commonly asked in interviews for academic programs are the same as those posed in job interviews, so it is a good idea to review those questions. Here are some additional questions typically asked of applicants to PhD programs:

- *Why have you chosen this program?*

Show your enthusiasm about studying in the program and explain why you believe it is the best place to develop your experience and skills. Make sure you can give a few specific reasons for applying for the particular program and how it will directly contribute to the development of your career.

- *Are you applying to other programs?*

If you are looking at other programs, you can be honest about that, but be sure to provide specific reasons that this program is the one for you.

• *What will you do if you are not accepted into our program?*

Make sure you have some kind of back-up plan to describe to the interviewer so that it is clear that you are the kind of person who is prepared for a change in circumstances.

• *What courses did you enjoy the most in your previous program?*

Talk about one or two classes you enjoyed that are directly related to your future course of study and give specific reasons you liked them.

• *How would you be able to contribute to our program? Why should we consider you for our program over other qualified candidates?*

Talk about skills and knowledge you have gained from course and fieldwork, as well as personal or professional characteristics that make you a particularly competitive candidate.

• *What do you believe to be the current issues in the academic or professional field? What do you think about (topic)?*

Make sure you are aware of current trends, issues and/or controversies in the field and be able to express your opinion on them.

Questions to Ask

Be aware that interviewers expect serious applicants to ask questions during the interview. However, you want to avoid questions about very general information that can easily be found on the institution's website. Presumably, you already know a great deal about the school and the program, and that is why you have chosen to apply there. Instead, listen to the interviewer and ask questions for more information about items of particular interest to you.

In addition to specific follow-up questions, it is a good idea to have a few questions prepared. Here are some examples:

- *What should I expect to work on during my first year?*
- *How long does it typically take to complete the program?*
- *Where are recent alumni employed?*
- *What is the selection timeline?*
- *What types of financial aid, scholarships or fellowships are available?*

Keep in mind that the reason you are being interviewed is that the school wants to know more about you than they can learn from just reading about you in your personal statement or résumé. They want to get a sense of who you are and if you are the right person to join their team. So, make sure to establish rapport with the interviewer and demonstrate your social skills. Even though you may be nervous, remember to:

• Be professional, but also show your personality. It is fine to smile and laugh at times.

• Be confident and sure of yourself, but not overconfident. Assume that while you are a qualified candidate, other good candidates are being interviewed by the school as well.

• Avoid simple yes or no answers. Answer questions completely, and then stop and wait for the next question.

Overall, the better informed you are about the program to which you are applying, as well as the faculty and their research, the better you will be able to ask pertinent questions. You can find key information from searching online and talking to others who are familiar with the program.

In Conclusion...

It is hoped that this guide has proven to be a useful resource for you – answering many of your most pressing questions about this exciting new journey and helping you to take this next step with greater confidence.

Although you'll undoubtedly encounter surprises and challenges along the way, studying in the U.S. may well be one of the most personally and professionally rewarding periods of your life. If you set your priorities, manage your time well, and stay organized, you will succeed academically; and if you are open to new experiences and actively engage with others around you, you will create friendships and memories that will last a lifetime. In the meantime, make sure to always take care of yourself, so you can make the most of your time here!

Above all, remember that you are not alone; from the time you are accepted to the day you graduate, the other students, faculty, and staff at your school are key sources of guidance and support. Don't be afraid to reach out and ask for help. Your success in the U.S. is a win for everyone. Good luck!

50863771R00095

Made in the USA
Lexington, KY
02 April 2016